Please renew/return this item by the last date shown.

So that your telephone call is charged at local rate, please call the numbers as set out below:

	From Area codes 01923 or 0208:	From the rest of Herts:
Renewals:	01923 471373	01438 737373
Enquiries:	01923 471333	01438 737333
Minicom:	01923 471599	01438 737599

L32b

2 6 AUG 2000

3 1 JAN 2002

1 2 JAN 2005

7 / 12

Hertfordshire
COUNTY COUNCIL

Community Information
Libraries

Please renew / return this item by the
last date shown.
Thank you for using your library.

L32

Harewood

HAREWOOD

The Life and Times of an English
Country House

Carol Kennedy

Hutchinson

London Melbourne Sydney Auckland Johannesburg

Hutchinson & Co. (Publishers) Ltd

An imprint of the Hutchinson Publishing Group

17–21 Conway Street, London W1P 6 JD

Hutchinson Group (Australia) Pty Ltd
30–32 Cremorne Street, Richmond South, Victoria 3121
PO Box 151, Broadway, New South Wales 2007

Hutchinson Group (NZ) Ltd
32–34 View Road, PO Box 40–086, Glenfield, Auckland 10

Hutchinson Group (SA) Pty Ltd
PO Box 337, Bergvlei 2012, South Africa

First published 1982
© Carol Kennedy 1982

Set in VIP Sabon by
D. P. Media Limited, Hitchin, Hertfordshire

Printed in Great Britain by The Anchor Press Ltd
and bound by Wm Brendon & Son Ltd,
both of Tiptree, Essex

British Library Cataloguing in Publication Data
Kennedy, Carol
    Harewood: The life and times of an English country
    house.
    1. Harewood House (England)—History
    I. Title
    942.8'19   DA664.H42

ISBN 0 09 146870 1

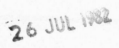

To my parents
Grace Kennedy and the late
Alan Kennedy, OBE, MD, FRCPI,
for their example of fortitude, loyalty
and perseverance

Contents

Illustrations

Acknowledgements

I gratefully acknowledge the help of the Earl and Countess of Harewood in enabling this book to be written, and the never-failing courtesy and assistance of Neville Ussher and his staff at the Harewood estate office. Special thanks are due also to Viscount Lascelles; to Barbara Baker, the Public Relations Officer at Harewood; to Mr J.M. Collinson, Leeds City Archivist; to Peter Goodchild, of the Institute of Advanced Architectural Studies at the University of York; to John Herbert, Press Officer at Christie's, and to the many residents of Harewood village and particularly the retired estate workers who gave generously of their time in helping me evoke memories of Harewood in earlier years.

Other owners of historic houses in Wharfedale were also immensely helpful, including Mr George Lane-Fox of Bramham Park, Mr and Mrs Sheepshanks of Arthington Hall and Colonel and Mrs Dawson of Weston Hall.

To Mary Mauchline, formerly Head of the History Department at Ripon College of Education, I owe much for the meticulous scholarship and ground-breaking research in her book *Harewood House*, published by David and Charles in 1970, particularly in its detailed account of the building and furnishing of the house.

Finally, a word of gratitude for the existence of the London Library, whose richly stocked shelves rarely failed to yield the most obscure work of history or topography, and whose staff were always helpful, courteous and knowledgeable.

Carol Kennedy
London, August 1981

1

'A Fortunate Place'

When George Henry Hubert Lascelles, seventh Earl of Harewood, wakes in his lofty, north-facing bedroom high up under the parapet of Harewood House, he can look out over a sweep of parkland and rolling West Yorkshire dale country outwardly little changed from the view that six generations of his forebears enjoyed. But his life is very different from theirs; different, even, from that of other English aristocrats of the late twentieth century who have come to terms with a changed social and economic fabric by going into business as restaurateurs, photographers or public relations consultants, and by opening their historic family homes to the public.

Lord Harewood is an internationally recognized figure in the world of music; his normal working week, when he is not travelling abroad, is spent in his office in the London Coliseum Theatre as full-time Director of the English National Opera, and his natural habitat is one of singers, conductors, contracts, gala openings, benefit nights and recording awards. This in itself is an unusual world for an English aristocrat to inhabit; doubly unusual for a member of the royal family, which George Harewood is by virtue of the fact that his father married the daughter of George V, making him first cousin to Elizabeth II.

The world of his ancestors, Harewood House and its estates in Wharfedale, is tucked into the weekends: it is an important part of his life, for he is a man who takes his lineal duties seriously, but it does not, for all that he runs the business side of it – the farm and the house-opening – as professionally as he does his opera company administration, sit naturally upon him. ' 'E doesn't take after 'is forebears at all,' as one old man in Harewood village stated with the faintest overtones of disapproval; 'they was all country people.'

Country people they may have been – the fifth earl, it's said in the village, 'did nothing for forty years but shoot rabbits' – but they came home from a day's sport with the Bramham Moor Hunt to an exquisite house crammed with treasures of European art and English craftsmanship. It was all part of an unbroken weave of life then for the moneyed county families. The present-day heir to Lascelles splendour occupies a modest suite of rooms on an upper floor, away from the Adam and Chippendale glories gazed on by visitors at £2 a head and parties of schoolchildren at special group prices.

Lord Harewood and his Australian second wife come home at weekends to a way of life that would have been as alien as moon walking to earlier generations of Lascelles; slipping quietly between the tourists in the great red-pillared Adam entrance hall, through a polished, heavy mahogany door at the far right corner that leads to the private family quarters. It is only in winter, for a couple of months when the Yorkshire weather keeps even the hardiest day-tripper away, that the Harewoods can enjoy the illusion of family life in the splendid yet intimately enchanting rooms which death duties, taxes and inflation have made as much a part of the local tourist industry as the fourteenth-century Minster or the railway museum in York. For the rest of the year, they inhabit a rambling set of rooms in what strikes a visitor as a curiously unreal, backstage part of the house, though the Harewoods themselves find it a comfortable retreat.

The two worlds are sharply differentiated once the mahogany door falls silently shut behind you. The private part of the house, which begins with the former main staircase to the bedroom floor, is hushed and distinctly warmer in winter than the rest; it has an air of being almost hermetically sealed. On dark days there is an immediate impression of aqueous gloom, with daylight filtering down the cavernous stairwell from a glass dome. The staircase, branching right and left into a double flight, is severe rather than elegant, its treads covered in dark red patterned carpet and its banisters, unexpectedly, of wrought iron. Off a landing at the top open four polished mahogany doors, two giving onto bedrooms and two to the oblong vestibule which forms the main entrance to the family flat, serving the double functions of hall and reception room. A few tapestry-covered chairs, a sofa and easy chairs cluster at one end on a dark blue patterned carpet; a gilded and carved frame holding family portrait miniatures hangs on the wall, and a Steinway baby grand stands by the front door. This is where the

Harewoods entertain their weekend guests to drinks before dinner, served by a butler from a butler's pantry (there are still vestiges of stately living). More often than not the guests are from the world of music – they usually put up the musicians who play at their winter chamber recitals in the gallery – and the Steinway is played by distinguished hands; Alfred Brendel had been there the week before my visit.

The vestibule has no windows and the initial subfusc impression can extend throughout the flat on all but the sunniest days. The sitting room and Lord Harewood's workroom, converted from one of the old state bedrooms and its dressing room, are lit by the small sash windows favoured by eighteenth-century architects to preserve the proportions of the façade. The view south over the terrace and lake is the finest the house offers, but the rooms, apart from those which retain their original function as the main bedrooms of the house, are modest in size, even by the standards of a converted family flat in London. A girl from Tyne Tees Television who came to arrange for the shooting of a documentary on the house complained that there was hardly room for the camera in the Harewoods' sitting room, which has a gold carpet, off-white sofa and chairs, and books piled on every available surface – volumes on travel, anthropology, music. There are a few good pictures, including a Piper and a fine Dutch landscape; a Leeds pottery horse, once the trade sign of a saddler's shop, stands in a niche among bookshelves (Lord Harewood collects Leeds ware). Lady Harewood runs the house and its domestic arrangements from a small bureau in this room. There is an open fire here in winter, but other splendid chimneypieces in the flat, including that in his Lordship's study, have cheap, old-fashioned electric fires stuck incongruously into them.

Lord Harewood's workroom, lit by one low-browed window, is crowded with books, stacked a dozen deep on the floor (the housekeeper has instructions not to move them) and rising on white-painted shelves to the ceiling, including a long run of music scores bound in blue buckram. A dust sheet covers the cluttered work table in his absence. An unexpected touch on the wall facing the window is a large painting of footballers done in bold, primitive style by a Lancashire artist named Roberts. Lord Harewood is a dedicated soccer fan and no mere figurehead as president of Leeds United Football Club. (Jackie Charlton, a personal friend of long standing, used Harewood House as one of the settings for a TV series called 'Best of British', in which the soccer star looked at various aspects of British life through the eyes of his upbringing as a miner's son.)

The flat rambles in all directions, a warren of anterooms and passages. A bare wooden back stairway disappears mysteriously into darkness. An electric lift ferries food and other supplies up from the ground floor. There is a modern kitchen with fitted yellow wall cabinets; in a passageway a large refrigerator lurks in an alcove behind a folding plastic screen. The domestic staff consists of a cook, a housekeeper, a butler and a live-in couple who do the cleaning. The Harewoods are here most weekends of the year except when abroad, but their longest stays are at Easter and Christmas, when the whole family foregathers for a week or ten days. The housekeeper, Olive Clarke, came in 1948 or 1949, before the house was opened to the public. She was the Princess Royal's head housemaid, with five girls working under her. She does not seem to mind her more modest role these days, but the dust, she says mildly, is terrible for settling everywhere.

The Harewoods' bedroom, known as the Red Bedroom, is always kept locked when they are away and has a special separate alarm system fitted to it. The main guest room is known as the White Bedroom – although in fact the dominant colour from the big four-poster bed is crimson – and the others are still called, as in the old days, the Rose Bedroom and the White Bedroom. Each has its bathroom and dressing room, and two other rooms can take an overflow of guests; the Harewoods can comfortably put up twelve people, which is the average size of their weekend house-parties, in contrast to the spacious pre-war days when twenty guests or more would sign the visitors' book at a time, often headed by royalty with their attendant equerries and ladies-in-waiting.

Harewood, then as now, was only one – if the richest in art treasures – of dozens of great country houses in this cushioned Yorkshire vale of the West Riding. It has always been a prosperous part of England. In 1548 the Bishop of Durham, writing to Henry VIII, described the area around Aberford, south of Wetherby, as the richest he had found in all his travels through Europe. Within ten miles of Hazelwood, the seat of the Vavasour family, situated between Leeds and Tadcaster, he had counted no fewer than 165 manor houses 'of Lords, Knights and Gentlemen of the best quality'. And within the West Riding, the twenty-mile stretch called Wharfedale, running from the Craven Hills in the west to Harewood in the east, offered particularly tempting sites for country houses with its green rises commanding wide views of the winding silver Wharfe.

An early nineteenth-century topographer listed the chief landowners of Wharfedale as William Myddelton of Myddelton Lodge, Sir Henry Carr Ibbetson of Denton Park, William Vavasour of Weston Hall, Walter Fawkes of Farnley Hall and the Earl of Harewood, adding that 'the beautiful seats of these Gentlemen are the first objects to catch the eye'. The seats still stand, although some have passed out of family ownership. Myddelton Lodge is now a hospital and Denton Park, once the home of Sir Thomas Fairfax, one of Cromwell's generals, and sold to the Carr Ibbetsons in the eighteenth century, is owned by a large electrical company which uses it as a technical training college. It is one of John Carr's Yorkshire masterpieces, with his characteristic octagon motif showing up in the twin towers at either end. Hazelwood Castle, for eight centuries the home of the Vavasours, is a Roman Catholic retreat house.

But on the whole, Wharfedale and the adjoining stretch of country around Wetherby are notable for the continuity of their landowning families, even if some have acquired accretions to the family name through marriage or a branch-line inheritance. There are still Lane-Foxes at Bramham Park, maintaining the hunting and other sporting tastes of their eighteenth-century squire forebears. Nicholas Horton-Fawkes farms a thousand acres around Farnley Hall, a stately pleasure dome decreed by Walter Fawkes in 1785 as the summer reception wing to his Jacobean manor house and designed by Carr as his last commission in Yorkshire. Thomas Girtin and William Turner came over here in the summer of 1796 from Harewood, where they were painting views of the house, and Turner became a close friend of Walter Fawkes, continuing for thirteen years to spend a month or six weeks of each summer here and endowing the house with scores of unique watercolours of itself and its setting, as well as of Turner's Continental travels.

So splendid was the collection that Walter Fawkes opened it, and his Grosvenor Place town house in Mayfair, to the public in 1819, pioneering in reverse the custom of today's owners of country mansions. The paintings, said the catalogue in lordly tones, would be found of interest 'to Patriot and Amateur alike'. In the intervening years some two hundred Turners have been sold by the family and only twenty-nine remain in the house – those of the house itself, its interior and local landscapes. Turner's bedroom, plain and relieved only by one of Carr's splendid chimneypieces, remains more or less as it was, looking east over the stable block. From the Octagon room – Carr's architectural trademark again – you can see in clear weather Harewood House to the left, about six miles away, and Ilkley to the right. Ruskin said of Farnley and its Turner association: 'Farnley Hall is unique, there is nothing like it in the world – a place where a great genius was loved and appreciated, who did all his best work for that place, and where it is treasured up like a monument in a shrine.'

The Fawkeses are one of the oldest families in Wharfedale, making the Lascelles, who came here from a little farther north in the county in 1739, look virtual parvenus. John Fawkes was Steward of the Forest of Knaresborough in 1340 and there has been a house continually on the site of Farnley Hall since that date. But even the Fawkeses pale in antiquity beside their cousins the Vavasours, who have been established in the neighbourhood of Otley as well as at Hazelwood for seven or eight hundred years, and whose Weston Hall is one of the very few houses of mainly Tudor construction left in this part of Yorkshire. (It was also, thanks to a wealthy ironmaster named Dawson whose family married into the Vavasours in 1833, one of the earliest houses in Yorkshire to have electricity, as well as a covered swimming pool in the park.) The present owner, the ironmaster's grandson, is Colonel Herbrand Vavasour Dawson, an authentic landowner with two thousand acres, mostly tenanted, and a grouse moor to his name, but whose daily way of life, at any rate through the long Yorkshire winter, would deter all but the hardiest aspirants to stately home ownership. Weston is paralysingly cold except for one small sitting room warmed by a coal fire; the Dawsons do not even attempt to heat the rest of the house and disarmingly explain; 'We run from room to room.' The Palladian Bramham Park, too, is bone-chilling: unusually for Yorkshire, where most great houses were built to face south, it looks to the north-east, and the March day I was there a small blizzard was blowing snow under the massive doors of the Great Hall. George Lane-Fox casually kicked a roll of sheets against it; in his small study a meagre electric fire barely took the edge off the frigid afternoon. These Yorkshire squires are made of hardy stuff and mostly seem to marry equally resilient wives, bred to northern draughts and cold corridors.

The exigencies of public opening to pay the upkeep have not yet caught up with all of them, but it's a close-run thing. Bramham Park, or about ten rooms of it, has been open to the public since 1953, shortly after Harewood. Weston is open 'on demand' to visitors as a condition of receiving grants as a Grade II listed building. Nicholas Horton-Fawkes was 'at a crossroads' in 1980, when he had to decide whether to open Farnley or not. His personal inclination was to keep it as a private family home, but the adjoining seventeenth-century manor with its smaller, oak-panelled rooms, carefully restored by the family, would obviously make more economical living quarters. Opening the Carr mansion, with its fine plasterwork and relics such as Cromwell's sword as well as the Turners, would solve the problem of the 'knife-edge' maintenance costs.

Most of these great houses were, and still are, linked by relationships, a spreading web of cousinage. Fawkeses are related to Vavasours, and the Sheepshanks of Arthington, a relatively new family who have lived at Arthington Hall for a mere 150 years, have a quirky connection with the Lascelles of Harewood. The story, as Charles Sheepshanks tells it, concerns Lady Mary Lascelles, daughter of the first earl, who decided that she wanted to marry a Sheepshanks. Her father is supposed to have said, 'I'm not having you marry someone with a damn silly name like Sheepshanks, get him to change it to Leeds or York or something like that.' So Lady Mary York she became, and her portrait as a young woman by John Hoppner hangs in the gallery at Harewood House. (In later life she grew immensely stout, and a more gruesome anecdote about her relates that when she was squeezed into her coffin in 1831 the sheer bulk of her burst the lead lining.)

With another old Wharfedale family, the Hawksworths, it was not cousinage or marriage which merged them into the Fawkes dynasty of Farnley (although they were distantly related), but a romantic story of virtue put to the test in the early eighteenth century. Young Francis Fawkes was the last male of his direct line, and in due course, if he had no sons, his estates were to pass to his cousin, a Vavasour of Weston. One day when Fawkes was out hunting and found himself near Weston Hall, he called in, wet and muddy, to his aunt's home hoping for rest and refreshment. Unfortunately, Mrs Vavasour was giving a dinner party that evening and hastily ushered her disreputable-looking nephew into the servants' hall for his meal. Angered by this snub, Fawkes immediately left Weston and rode across the valley to his mother's kinsmen at Hawksworth Hall, where he was given a very different reception. As in some biblical parable, he was given grouse and fresh trout to eat and the best room in the house was made ready for him. Not only that, but the Hawksworths gladly lent him the then enormous sum of three hundred guineas which Fawkes had the notion of asking as clinching proof of their friendship. Three months later he returned the bag of gold unopened, and when he died without children in 1786 it was found that he had made over all the Fawkes estates to Walter Hawksworth and cut the Vavasours completely out of the inheritance. So anxious was he to ensure that they did not succeed to any of the Fawkes fortune that it is said he made twenty-five different wills in as many years, each stipulating the same conditions. The Hawksworths took the name of Fawkes, though the family house continued to be known as Hawksworth Hall; it is now a home for the care of spastics.

Most of these great West Yorkshire families – Fawkes, Hawksworth, Vavasour, Lascelles – have Norman origins and can trace their antecedents back to the Conquest, though the Lascelles line was complex and many-branched before Henry Lascelles came to Wharfedale in 1739 from Northallerton. Large portions of Yorkshire, then mainly wasteland with a few pockets of cultivated country, were given by William of Normandy to his compatriots who had fought with him at Hastings, and one of these, Robert de Romelli, was given Harewood together with Skipton-in-Craven and some other big estates. Harewood lay in one of the fertile areas, situated on a high ridge of the native millstone grit overlooking the Wharfe valley, and with soil of superior quality to the clay farther west towards Harrogate. In the nineteenth century it was to be described by the topographer T.D. Whitaker as 'a fortunate place, blessed with much natural beauty and fertility'. The village itself stands almost midway between Leeds and Harrogate, its crest of land falling away steeply towards Otley and Harrogate in a great curve of road known as Harewood Bank; when the road was first asphalted early this century the horses had to be fitted with rubber shoes to prevent them from slipping. It also stands almost exactly in the middle of England between the Irish Sea and the North Sea, and in the eighteenth century was a busy intersection for stagecoach traffic, with as many as twenty-two stages rolling through it each day. Today, its position on the main A61 highway from Leeds to Harrogate ensures a hectic torrent of commuter cars morning and evening, often going dangerously fast down Harewood Bank.

The name of Harewood has been given a variety of derivations, from the straightforward 'hare's wood' to the Anglo-Saxon *haerh*, meaning a temple or place of meditation. The site of the present church has certainly been associated with religious activity far earlier than its Norman founding. The late Canon H.H. Griffith of Harewood, whose hobby was researching the history of his parish, believed there was a church of some kind as early as AD 830 – probably a humble structure of wattle and daub, in which a saintly priest called Farmon ministered to the needs of the people and made the translation of St Matthew's Gospel which is now in the Bodleian Library. In old documents the name is customarily spelled Harwood, but West Yorkshire people always use the long 'a' as in 'hare', regarding the 'har' pronunciation as southern affectation. The latter, nevertheless, is the accepted, 'correct' style for the Lascelles family title and the house.

In the mid-nineteenth century, John Jones in his *History and Antiquities of Harewood* remarked how the traveller or visitor 'is generally struck with the regularity and beauty of the village' as it had been laid out by John Carr to complete his grand design for the house. It remains much the same today, consisting of two main roads crossing at a T junction, bordered with Georgian terraced cottages of severely formal elegance in local stone and, on the Wetherby road, known as the Avenue where it forms the stem of the T, with long gardens running down to the pavement. Jones made a point of mentioning the fine trees shading these gardens; in photographs from the 1920s the stately elms almost meet over the Avenue in their full summer foliage, but disease began to fell them and the destruction was completed by the great gale of March 1962 which also decimated Lancelot 'Capability' Brown's woodscape around Harewood House. Not one of the Avenue's elms is left today, and the once-colourful flower gardens have been mostly planted to vegetables, but Harewood is still recognizably the place it has been for two hundred years, with vestiges of an even older self in the rambling lanes behind Carr's terraces, in the church with its Norman font and fine medieval tombs, and in the two broken towers of the castle rising out of the trees on Harewood Bank. The farming land, too, is as good as it has been for nine centuries, and the village has kept relatively immune from the population drain which has taken the heart's blood out of so many English rural communities since 1920.

As early as 1086, twenty years after the Conquest, Harewood's valuation in the Domesday survey showed that its fertility had not escaped the attentions of the taxman. The entry in Bawden's translation of

Domesday runs: 'In Harewood with Berewicks, Tor, Sprot and Grim had ten carucates of land to be taxed. Land to five ploughs. Forty shillings.' This is the first authentic information we have of Harewood; Tor, Sprot and Grim, who sound like sinister Norse trolls, were Saxon chieftains who owned three manors in the area. A carucate was not an exact measure of land but was calculated on the basis of how much a plough might, in the normal course of husbandry, till in a year; estimates varied under different reigns, running from sixty to a hundred acres in the time of Richard I and a century later, under Edward I, rising to 180 acres. It embraced all types of land, woodland and pasture as well as arable. John Jones comments crisply that 'these unfortunate Saxons, falling within the grasp of the Conqueror, appear to have been wholly disseized of this fair domain. . . . William seems to have visited Yorkshire with more severity than any other part of England.'

Robert de Romelli did well out of William's generosity, for at the time of Domesday, Harewood manor alone comprised eight townships (Harewood, Alwoodley, East Keswick, Weardley, Wigton, Wike, Dunkeswick and Weston) spreading over 12,180 acres or more than nineteen square miles. So well cultivated was the land that more than two out of every three acres were bearing crops. It was one of the richest manorial prizes in England. Not surprisingly, Robert's only daughter Cecily made a good marriage with the Earl of Chester, William de Meschines, who brought with him a substantial slice of Cumberland to add to the Harewood estates. (Henry I granted the family all the land lying between the rivers Duddon and Derwent and between the lakes of Bassenthwaite and Derwentwater.)

Both the sons of this marriage, Rafe and Matthew, died without children, so the two daughters, Alice and Avicia, became joint heiresses and kept their name even after their respective marriages to Fitz Duncan, Earl of Murray, the nephew of Duncan I of Scotland, and William de Curci, Steward of the Royal Household to Henry I. Alice inherited the Skipton lands while Harewood went to Avicia and her husband. It was William de Curci who made extensive improvements to Harewood's magnificently situated castle in the twelfth century, and he is also reputed to have been the builder of the Norman church in 1116, according to a carved beam which was found when the building was restored in 1793, but of which no trace now remains.

The son of Alice and Fitz Duncan created a Wharfedale legend by drowning in the river where it forms a narrow chasm in Bolton

Woods. He had often jumped the four-foot-wide gap when out on walks with his dog, the story goes, but on this occasion the greyhound held back suddenly on the leash, causing the boy to lose his footing and fall into the fast current. The tale formed the basis of a poem by Wordsworth, among others ('The boy is in the arms of Wharfe. . .'), and is traditionally supposed to have been the reason why Alice moved the priory dedicated to the Virgin Mary and St Cuthbert, which had been endowed by her parents, from Embsay to Bolton Woods.

Harewood remained in the de Curci family for another three generations. In 1205 King John granted his Chamberlain, Waryn Fitz Gerald, who was married to Avicia's granddaughter Alice, 'free warren' in Harewood – the sole right to kill game on the estate, which would otherwise have been considered royal property under the forest laws dating from the Norman Conquest. He was also granted the right to hold a fair there each year on the first three days of July, and a market every Monday for the sale of agricultural produce. The fair continued for several centuries under different lords of the manor and was held on the site of what became the Harewood blacksmith's forge and today is its petrol station.

The Fitz Geralds' only daughter, Margery, married as her first husband Baldwin de Redvers, sixth Earl of Devon, and from the Redvers family, by inheritance and marriage, the Harewood estates passed successively to the Earls of Albemarle and Holderness; Edmund Plantagenet (Crouchback), the son of Henry III; Lord L'Isle of Rougemont and William de Aldburgh, who obtained permission in 1365 to fortify his manor house and proceed to rebuild the castle in its final form. The Aldburgh family motto, 'Vat Sal Be Sal' ('What Shall Be, Shall') is still visible in the twentieth-century ruins, carved over what used to be the portcullised main gateway on the east side; as are the Aldburgh arms and those of Edward Baliol, King of Scotland, on either side of the entrance. Sir William was a Messenger to the King, a civil service post of high rank and responsibility, and the friendship between the two families may have been the factor which saved Harewood Castle from the Scottish raids which wrought great damage to other buildings in the area and elsewhere in Yorkshire, including even Harewood's Norman church.

The castle must have been an awesome sight in its fourteenth-century heyday. It was certainly one of the most impressively sited in England, built at the head of a long slope above the southern bank of the Wharfe and commanding spectacular views across the valley to horizons bounded by the Craven Hills to the north-west and York to the east. It was a four-square structure of freestone walls averaging seven feet in t⁻ickness, arranged roughly in the shape of a parallelogram with a square tower at each corner, two of them over a hundred feet high. As befitted its daunting appearance, it was the focal point of a feudal domain over which the lord of the manor had literally the power of life and death. Gallows Hill, now a gentle rise behind the Harewood Arms hotel, was the place of summary execution for malefactors; the Great Hall of the castle was used as a court of justice and the right of lords of the manor to inflict the death penalty only fell into disuse when circuit judges began to tour the country districts. Inside, the formidable aspect of the fortress would have been softened by rich and colourful furnishings, heraldic carvings and stained glass. The will of Margery de Aldburgh in 1391 enumerated bequests of silver and silver-gilt vessels, tapestries, beds with embroidered coverlets in crimson, green and gold, a red-painted chest, scarlet cushions and a quantity of gowns and furred cloaks in predominant shades of red.

William de Aldburgh died childless and his two sisters Sybil and Elizabeth inherited Harewood. Both married into old and distinguished Yorkshire families, the Rythers and the Redmans; Elizabeth's husband, Sir Richard Redman, became Speaker of the House of Commons in 1415. The two families seem to have enjoyed a very amicable and practical arrangement; for more than two hundred years, from 1390 to 1630, they lived in the castle either alternately or together, keeping their manorial possessions entire and undivided. Descendants of the Redmans held Harewood for seven generations, those of the Rythers for nine. The Redmans, meanwhile, married several times into the Gascoigne family, whose estate bordered Harewood and whose home was a medieval manor house called Gawthorp Hall. Its situation was about 350 yards south of where Harewood House now stands, and its foundations, for it was pulled down by Edwin Lascelles in 1759 to build his fine new mansion, lie under Capability Brown's lake in the park.

At some stage the fortunes of the two families merged and the Gascoignes became lords of the manor of Harewood as well as Gawthorp, a process which probably started when Matthew Redman, the last of his family to live in Harewood Castle, married a daughter of Sir William Gascoigne in the mid-sixteenth century but died without issue. The Ryther half of the inheritance is thought to have been sold either to the

Redmans or the Gascoignes. In any case, the estates eventually came together in Queen Elizabeth's reign under Margaret Gascoigne, who married Thomas Wentworth and whose grandson was to become the ill-fated Earl of Strafford, impeached and beheaded for treason during the Long Parliament of Charles I. Gascoignes had long been people of consequence in the realm; another Norman family, they had produced in Henry IV's time a famous Chief Justice of England, Sir William Gascoigne, who figured in Shakespeare's *Henry IV, Part II* for his legendary act of courage in committing Henry V when Prince of Wales to prison for contempt of court – a story which disappointingly is given short shrift by historians ('demonstrably untrue', says the *Dictionary of National Biography*). Shakespeare has the King say: 'Happy am I that have a man so bold/That dares do justice to my proper son;/And not less happy, having such a son/That would deliver up his greatness so/Into the hands of justice.'

Gawthorp Hall, judging by a print of 1722, was a commodious house with chapel, stables and outbuildings, pleasure gardens and orchards, all enclosed by a wall. By the time the print was executed, it had evidently been remodelled in Queen Anne style, two-storeyed with a massive pedimented entrance and a paved terrace along the front. It was undoubtedly a more comfortable home to live in than Harewood Castle, and its charms as a retreat from the then harsh and risky world of public life and politics are poignantly recorded by the Earl of Strafford, by nature a country-loving squire. In August 1624, he wrote from Gawthorp: 'Our harvest is all in, a most fine season to make fishponds; our plums all gone and past; peaches, quinces and grapes almost fully ripe. . . . These only we country men muse of, hoping in such harmless retirements for a just defence from the higher powers. . . .' Alas for Strafford, there was to be no such defence, and the higher powers would have his head in the end.

Again in 1636, newly returned from administering Ireland as Lord Lieutenant, he wrote to Archbishop Laud (also doomed to be impeached and executed) from his Yorkshire retreat: 'Lord! With what quietness in myself could I live here, in comparison of that noise and labour I meet with elsewhere; and, I protest, put more crowns in my purse at the year's end, too.' His last thoughts on the scaffold were of his distant home at Harewood and the dependants he must leave there: 'Next, Lord, we commend unto Thee that family, that house which is now ready to be left desolate, that wife which by and by shall want a husband, those children which by and by shall want a father, those servants which by and by shall want a master. . . .'

Strafford's son William inherited Gawthorp, Harewood Castle and the rest of the estates but in 1656 was forced by financial exigency to sell them to two eminent London businessmen, Sir John Lewis and Sir John Cutler, a member of the Grocers' Company. The price stipulated for the main portion of the estate was £25,347 18s. 8d., which included seven good-sized townships. The purchase agreement filled more than fifty folios, itemizing most of the individual farms, the fields with their titles and acreages and the names of the tenants. Lord Strafford was so impoverished after his father's execution that he asked Cutler for an advance of £1000 on the deal in April 1658.

Sir John Cutler – no one seems to have heard of his partner Lewis again – has gone down in folklore as a miser and a hard landlord, satirized mercilessly by Pope in *Moral Essays* ('Cutler saw tenants break and houses fall,/For very want, he could not build a wall'), but the reputation may have been undeserved. He certainly made some large charitable endowments, and on a personal level was regarded as good coffee-house company by that most companionable of men, Samuel Pepys, who remarked that 'his discourse was well worth hearing'. One of the things he was blamed for at Harewood was aiding the destruction of the castle by using it as a source of building materials for cottages – an unfair accusation in view of the terms of the bill of sale. One old cottage in the back lanes of Harewood village is still known as Cutler's Cottage and is reputed to be built of stone from the castle; it bears the carved initials J.C. over the doorway and is now the home of an insurance executive with a taste for collecting antiquarian maps of the area. A later lord of the manor attempted to use the castle stone for repairing farm buildings, but found the mortar and cement so compacted by age that it was easier to procure new stone from the quarry.

On Cutler's death the estates went to his only surviving daughter Elizabeth, Countess of Radnor, with the stipulation that if she had no children they should pass on her death to John Boulter, a Cutler kinsman. This duly happened in 1696 and Boulter appears to have redeemed Cutler's unfortunate reputation in the neighbourhood, being described by the historian Camden in 1731 as

a Person very generous and charitable, hath been a considerable Benefactor to the Church and Poor of his Parish; for ever since he hath come to this Estate, he hath allowed a considerable sum to the Vicar for preaching every

Lord's Day in the Afternoon, and catechising the Children; and another to a School-master in the Town to teach the poor Children Reading, Writing and Arithmetick gratis.

It was Boulter's son Edmund who was forced by debt to sell the manor and all its appurtenances in 1739 to Henry Lascelles, a former Collector of Customs in Barbados, Member of Parliament for Northallerton and soon to be a London merchant banker.

The village to which Lascelles moved his household was a sprawling, lively market centre extending up a winding lane to the church, which nowadays sits enclosed in a copse within the park surrounding Harewood House. The parish church of All Saints was already famous in Lascelles's time. It was a square-towered building in Perpendicular style which had undergone complete rebuilding in the reign of Edward III and further extensive alterations in the fifteenth century; the only trace remaining of William de Curci's Norman structure being the fine stone font with its cable moulding. It was to be drastically 'restored' again in 1793, when much fine medieval stained glass, carved oak seats and an ancient pulpit were lost (as well as the carved beam giving de Curci as the church's founder), and finally in 1862 to receive the ministrations of Sir George Gilbert Scott, architect of the Albert Memorial and St Pancras Station, and high priest of Victorian Gothic.

The splendidly carved tombs with their full-length effigies, still arguably the finest of any parish church in England, date from between 1400 and 1500; there are six, including those of Sir William Gascoigne, the youthful-looking Lord Chief Justice, in his stone robes, who was buried here four years after Agincourt, and knightly Redmans and Rythers with their ladies. De Curci is reputedly buried in a side chapel. After 1795 the Lascelles would join this ancient company, generation after generation of them being buried in a family vault, up to the Princess Royal in 1965. Humbler members of the estate 'family' were not forgotten; there is an inscription in the church to Samuel Popplewell, who died in September 1780 aged sixty-seven after more than thirty years' service as Edwin Lascelles's steward – 'which office he executed with great integrity and distinguished abilities' – and in the churchyard to John Jewell, porter at Harewood House for nearly thirty years, who died in September 1823 aged fifty. Jewell filled his plentiful free time between showing the occasional visitors round by compiling the first comprehensive guidebook to the house; by 1859, when John Jones published his history of Harewood, it was already a rare collectors' item.

In the village itself, up to the mid-seventeenth century, had stood a market house or toll booth with six butchers' shops underneath – a local amateur historian has sited it in the centre of the Wetherby road close to its junction with the Leeds–Harrogate highway. This structure was still standing in 1656, as it is mentioned in Strafford's bill of sale, but it was probably pulled down soon afterwards. Also in the Wetherby road, close by, was the old market cross, on whose broad steps the farmers of the district used to sell their butter, hens and eggs. This was not demolished until 1804 when the slope of the road was levelled. Bear-baiting and football were popular village pastimes, and the big annual event was the October sheep fair, held on the second and last Mondays of that month; this continued to be of growing importance in the village economy up to the middle of the nineteenth century.

But Harewood's early history had not been exclusively agricultural: ironworks flourished in the area from the thirteenth century and iron-stone was being dug in the neighbourhood of Kirkby Overblow in the reign of King John. Knaresborough was a thriving centre of iron forging by about 1230 and fifty years later the forges at Swindon and Kirkby Overblow were commanding high rents. In the Harewood accounts for the eighth to the ninth year of Edward I's reign, the farm on one forge alone is returned at £38 5s., while the value of iron ore sold is set down at 18s. Two years later, two forges are mentioned, one appraised at £39 17s. 6d. and the other at £16 6s. 11d. There was also lead mining in Upper Wharfedale, an industry which continued to prosper in the dales up to the late nineteenth century, when the discovery of rich veins in Nevada reduced the world price of lead and made the Yorkshire seams uneconomic to work. The Duke of Devonshire owned the royal-ties to the lead mines of Upper Wharfedale, the most important of which were at Grassington and Hebden.

Also important, from about the twelfth century, were the linked trades of spinning, weaving and dyeing which were brought into the area by Flemish immigrants; the parish registers of Harewood are filled with entries for stuff weavers, linen weavers, cloth weavers and wool combers. Harewood was also noted for a while for the manufacture of ribbons, and about 1755 Edwin Lascelles built a handsome block on the Wetherby road as a ribbon manufactory, perhaps as a scheme to relieve unemployment. It did not last long, however, and the building with its distinctive half-moon-shaped upper windows became four cottages, and remains the same today.

From the middle of the eighteenth century, the industrial revolution began to gather pace in the West Riding. The rich Yorkshire coalfield embraced about one-third of the district, extending to a few miles north of Leeds, and the rivers Aire, Swale, Ure, Wharfe and Calder were to add their stored-up energy to the impetus of the new technology, with the weaving industry being taken over first by water-powered mills and then by steam. But as the tide of industrialization rose, Harewood remained primarily an island of agriculture. By 1859, John Jones remarked, 'its appearance is so thoroughly rural that it might be 100 miles away instead of standing on the confines of one of the busiest manufacturing districts in the world. The neighbourhood is remarkable for its salubrity and its pure and bracing air.' Many of its inhabitants, he noted, lived to a great age for the labouring classes of that time, or any time – well into their nineties. With the medicinal springs of Harrogate already, at the beginning of the seventeenth century, being advertised to the world by a Dr Stanhope of York, who published a pamphlet on the subject entitled *Cures Without Care*, and with London soon to be only a few days' travel away by the improved stagecoach services and fast turnpike roads, it was clearly an attractive place for a merchant banker/politician with local roots and London ambitions to plant his family tree.

2

A Family Builds Its Fortune

Throughout most of the eighteenth and nineteenth centuries, until an agricultural slump combined with the rise of other forms of capital investment began to drive money elsewhere, land was the dominant factor in the balance sheet of British wealth. Only the big overseas trading companies could rival the great landed estates in terms of return on capital invested. At the beginning of the eighteenth century 'the landed interest', commonly defined as landowners and farmers, disposed of roughly half the total wealth of the nation, though comprising less than one-fifth of the families of England and Wales. Rent alone from the 25 million acres of cultivated land in England and Wales in the first decade of the century added up to £11 million, about one-quarter of the entire national income.

The acquisition of land was a passport to wealth and influence. In most eighteenth-century Parliaments about two-thirds of the members of the House of Commons were landowners of greater or lesser degree, and it was the ambition of every entrepreneur who made a fortune out of the lucrative colonial trade or supply contracts for the armed forces to enter the ranks of the landed gentry, through marriage or purchase or both. Government ministers were actually expected to make money out of public office (unlike the Victorian ideal of noble disinterest which still, if slightly cracked and brittle, governs our political morality today), and with that money they bought country estates and built minor palaces on them. Sir Robert Walpole built Houghton Hall in Norfolk and George Lyttelton, a junior court official who later became Chancellor of the Exchequer, was able in the 1750s to rebuild his family home, Hagley Hall in Worcestershire, in Palladian grandeur.

The gentry formed a deep band just below the couple of hundred peers at the top of the social and economic pyramid; there were perhaps up to 20,000 gentry families, ranging from those of baronets and knights down to mere 'esquires' and gentlemen. Their incomes ranged from £1000 to £4000 a year, compared with £10,000 or £12,000 for the great landlords, while the grandest of the dukes and senior earls, one historian has estimated, were enjoying incomes approaching £50,000 by the end of the century and were richer than many of Continental Europe's small independent princes.

The landed proprietors grew wealthier on rising rents as the century progressed and the spread of the enclosure system made farmland and tenanted estates more profitable – and they spent on an ever-increasing scale. They engaged the services of eminent architects and landscape gardeners to crown their estates with a fittingly majestic house and park, though many preferred to be their own architects, employing master masons and carpenters to give shape to their ideas. They established town houses in London designed, as Matthew Brettingham had shown the way with Norfolk House in St James's Square, for the more social mode of life which was developing. The richer young bloods made extensive tours of Europe in pursuit of cultivated taste and returned with quantities of paintings, porcelain and fine Continental furniture. By the 1790s, there were an estimated four hundred families who could be classed as great landlords, both inside and outside the nobility. They owned anything from 5000 to 50,000 acres, had an average income of £10,000 a year, and their country houses formed a social hub for the district, provided the principal source of employment and were often centres of political influence as well.

Most of these glittering prospects lay far in the future for Henry Lascelles's eldest son Edwin, but the father had no doubt that land was where he wanted to invest the considerable wealth he had inherited from his family's trading activities in the West Indies and which he had amassed on his own account as a merchant and Collector of Customs in Barbados. The latter was an occupation in which considerable money could be made, often by dubious methods, and Henry Lascelles received his share of accusations of corruption, some of which went on reverberating long after he had returned to England in 1739, bought his country estate and set up the West India merchant house of Lascelles and Maxwell in Mark Lane in the City of London. In fact Lascelles's purchase of a parliamentary borough, Northallerton, in 1745 was largely motivated by the desire to exert leverage on American attempts being made to bring legal action against him and his brother Edward, who followed him as Collector of Customs.

Lascelles seems to have achieved his purpose – at least, no action was brought – and he was equally fortunate, or shrewd, in managing to acquire a suitable country estate. Very little property was changing hands at the time, and for most aspirants to the gentry there was only one way in – marriage. Lascelles, already married (for the second time) to a Barbados lady, and with two sons, Edwin and Daniel, born in the island, did not have that option open to him. He found just the right property, however, in the connecting lands of Gawthorp and Harewood, which were being sold by the Boulters to clear their debts. The two estates with their townships and tenants and the manor house itself, Old Gawthorp Hall, were valued for sale at £63,827. The estate was ideally situated; within easy reach of Northallerton and the North Riding, where the Lascelles had long-established roots, and only eight miles from the burgeoning new industrial centre of Leeds. It was also within twenty miles of York with all its fashionable diversions of shops, assembly room and the new racecourse. There was even a satisfying genealogical link; an earlier Lascelles in the time of Charles I had married a Miss Frances St Quentin who was connected with the Aldburgh and Gascoigne families; both had once lorded it over Harewood.

The Lascelles themselves could claim to be one of the oldest Yorkshire families and, like so many others, sprang from Norman stock, apparently deriving their name from a village in Normandy called Lassele. A knight called Picot de Lascelles from this village commanded part of the Norman army at the Battle of Hastings and is mentioned in the Domesday Book as displacing the three Saxon lords who had formerly owned Scruton in North Yorkshire – doubtless another of William's freely scattered rewards to his followers. The first of the Harewood line turns up in the records in 1315; John de Lascelles of Hinderskelfe, in the North Riding, where Castle Howard now stands. He may have been a younger son of the Sowerby and Brackenburgh branch of the family, whose arms are the same. The Northallerton connection began in the early 1600s, through marriage with a girl from that district.

From medieval times the family had been a mildly distinguished one in public service, holding office as justices of the peace, sheriffs and Members of Parliament. Francis Lascelles, great-grandfather of Henry, served in Cromwell's army as a colonel in the Civil War and was appointed to sit on the commission charged with trying Charles I. He attended twelve sittings, but whether from conscience or prudence stayed away on the day that sentence of death was passed on the king; neither did he sign the warrant. When the monarchy was restored, his republican past was conveniently forgotten and he was returned as a Member of Parliament three times under Charles II.

The family had been connected prosperously with Barbados for nearly half a century before Henry Lascelles returned to England in 1739. The following year he set up his merchant bank in partnership with George Maxwell, a sugar planter who had served under him in Bridgetown as searcher of the customs. The business of the new house (which continued, under the name of Wilkinson and Gaviller, until its offices off Great Tower Street were destroyed in the huge bombing raid of 29 December 1940) lay chiefly in financing loans to planters, negotiating their sales in England on commission, and arranging for supplies of various kinds to be sent out to the West Indies – anything from hoops for sugar casks to a spinet for a planter's home.

In fact the range of activities undertaken by these houses, the forerunners of many of today's merchant banks, was amazingly diverse, often requiring the personal judgement of the partners on their clients' family matters. In order to facilitate the consignment of crops and supplies, they had to hold shares in ships; planters also did this, and in some cases ships were entirely owned by planters and merchants in the islands, who thereby gained priority in shipping their commodities. Factoring houses like Lascelles and Maxwell invested money for their clients; represented them in their dealings with government departments; ordered machinery to their specifications; dealt with suppliers of unsatisfactory goods; and sometimes became involved in law-suits on their clients' behalf. On one occasion, recounted by the historian Richard Pares, Lascelles and Maxwell undertook to keep an eye out for a suitable parliamentary seat for a friend with political ambitions who commanded the squadron on the Jamaica station.

In his essay 'A London West India Merchant House', published in 1961, Pares gives a fascinating glimpse of the variety of commissions executed by the Lascelles firm in two typical months, September and October 1743, shortly after Maxwell had become a partner. For various clients they bought lottery tickets, ordered a copy of Gay's *Fables*, had a gown dyed and a bell re-cast, interviewed a milliner to complain of the poor quality of the fur trimming on a nightgown, checked personally on a son's progress at school, placed orders for beef, candles, tongue, claret and Dutch clinkers, and instructed a coppersmith about a special commission.

Besides this day-to-day variety, there were certain staple duties, including insurance of the homeward-bound sugar consignments and the outward-bound stores. For this they would go to one of the public companies such as the London Assurance, with which Lascelles and Maxwell had an open account, settling once a year. The factoring houses were also responsible for hiring skilled workers or professional employees required in the colony; it might be a doctor, a book-keeper or a plumber. (In the latter case the firm encountered some difficulty, being told bluntly that no good workman would leave England to go to the West Indies unless he were 'a Person in debt'. Some were reluctant to go anyway, fearing they would be 'put to the hard labour of Negroes' or that the climate would be too trying.)

One of the more tiresome occupational hazards must have been looking after the children of their island clients. At different times the partners might have to decide whether to supply some youth with money in order to release him from the clutches of moneylenders, to deal with an obstreperous schoolboy faced with expulsion, or to control the extravagance of undergraduates living it up at Oxford. Two did in fact have to be shipped home to Barbados in disgrace at a cost of £2220.

Such eclectic and unpredictable services required considerable reserves of capital. At least £20,000 was needed for paying the freight charges and duties on sugar consignments alone, and for accepting the bills of exchange drawn on them by the planters. Many planters also wanted substantial loans and advances upon their accounts. Some factors required mortgages to underwrite these, but Lascelles and Maxwell were content with less security than other firms demanded; they would allow debts to run into thousands without asking for a bond or mortgage. One client ran up debts of more than £14,000 without being asked to provide security. Indeed, the house once actually refused to pay bills of exchange for a planter who was understood to be mortgaging his plantation, taking the view that a mortgage would destroy his credit in the island.

Later on in the firm's history, however, mortgages became more frequent and, if unwillingly, Lascelles and Maxwell occasionally found themselves taking over a debtor's property. In 1836, when slave owners received compensation for the abolition of their human assets, the heirs of Henry Lascelles were recorded as owning four plantations and 933 slaves in Barbados and two plantations and 344 slaves in Jamaica. Sugar and slaves, as the present Lord Harewood allows, were the commodities on which his family built its fortune, though under the circumstances of the time it was inevitable that some of the money it advanced would go to purchase slaves. The slave merchants in Liverpool and Bristol expected the London financial houses to provide security on behalf of the colonial slave dealers. Large sums were involved – £10,000 was not unusual as surety that the local slave trader complied with the conditions laid down by the ship-owners. Besides this type of business, on which a London house would receive the usual 5 per cent interest, factors also loaned substantial sums to the island traders for the outright purchase of slaves, some of whom were then shipped to other islands or to Carolina.

Huge debts were run up by these slave merchants; one man and his son between them owed Lascelles and Maxwell £75,000 and the Harvie family of Jamaica at one time owed £80,000. By the middle 1760s, the house was owed at least £120,000 by West India merchants. Henry Lascelles's personal fortune helped the firm sustain debts of this size; although George Maxwell was credited in the company's books with half the capital in the form of debts and credits, it is not recorded that he brought any money of his own into the business, and in his will referred to Lascelles as his 'dear friend and benefactor'. After 1750, when he handed over his partnership to his younger son Daniel, Lascelles continued to invest in Barbados by lending on his own account to the planters, and remained the mainstay of the firm's liquidity. When Lascelles made a loan himself, he only had to sell his own securities, whereas when the firm advanced money it often had to take up outside resources – probably from Lascelles himself. When Lascelles died in 1753, leaving one-third of his £284,000 fortune to Daniel, the business came under severe financial pressure and frequently operated on a bank overdraft.

As early as 1740, the year after he had bought the Harewood and Gawthorp estates, Lascelles had put his eldest son Edwin, born in 1712, in charge of them while he concentrated on building up the business in London. By 1748, Edwin was already being described as Lord of the Manor of Harewood in the parish registers; on his father's death he inherited £166,666 and shortly afterwards made his decision to build an elegant new house. While he was planning the project and thinking about suitable architects, a major event took place in the normally

placid life of Harewood, and Edwin Lascelles's reaction to it demonstrated a characteristic resolution and pugnacity. The Turnpike Trusts,
which had been set up by Parliament in the previous century, empowered certain private citizens to make and maintain stretches of highway
and to levy tolls at specific points on all who used them. The trusts and
the toll system were widely detested and nowhere more so than in Yorkshire, though one of the roadmakers who worked for the trusts, John
Metcalf, known as Blind Jack of Knaresborough, was a local folk-hero:
still making roads when he was past seventy, Metcalf was a familiar
figure as he strode up hills and along valley bottoms, always alone,
prodding the ground with his long staff as he planned where bridges and
culverts should go and how an embankment should be constructed to
withstand winter flooding. It was an astonishing achievement for a
blind man and many of the roads he made, including that from Harrogate to Harewood, endured until the coming of the motor vehicle.
But some years before Metcalf began his work, the setting up of the
toll-houses and gates had roused communities in Yorkshire to violent
fury. At Selby, the town crier went round calling on the townspeople to
bring axes and crowbars to smash the offending barrier; a great deal of
damage was done and the military were called out to restore order.

In the summer of 1753, a large group of men from the manufacturing
districts around Leeds, who had already been responsible for destroying
toll barriers at Halton Dial on the York road, at Beeston and on the
Leeds–Bradford road, sent word to Edwin Lascelles that they intended
to demolish the toll bar near Harewood Bridge. Lascelles decided to
confront them personally and on 25 June 1753 he advanced at the head
of about eighty of his estate tenants and workmen, all well armed, to
meet some three hundred men carrying swords and clubs. The
encounter took place in a field called Hill Green; many men were
wounded on both sides but Lascelles eventually succeeded in taking
thirty of the rioters prisoner, ten of whom were subsequently committed
to detention in York Castle. The mob, according to a contemporary
historian, was 'greatly exasperated at the defeat, and they threatened to
pull down Gawthorp Hall'. Dragoons were summoned from York and
quartered at Harewood to keep the peace, but they were soon summoned to quell a worse riot at Briggate in Leeds, where five hundred
demonstrators were involved. The Riot Act was read but disregarded,
and the soldiers were at last ordered to fire. They fired first with blank
powder charges and then with live musket balls, killing eight and

wounding fifty, many of whom later died from their injuries; from then on there were no more turnpike riots.

This unwonted excitement over, Harewood relapsed into its customary peaceful agricultural routine and its lord of the manor returned to the more agreeable task of designing his new pleasure grounds and mansion. He was highly delighted with his father's choice of land; the gentle southern slope of Harewood Bank, rising above the Old Hall, offered the perfect site for a house with wide views over Wharfedale; woods and water abounded and the Stank Beck, in the hollow where the old house stood, plunged suddenly into a narrow ravine, giving sufficient force to turn a millwheel and, eventually, to be dammed to make Capability Brown's splendid lake. Even the Gothic ruin which contemporary fashion required to set off a classically designed mansion was ready to hand in the authentically decaying outline of Harewood Castle on the crest beyond the medieval church.

The advantages were more than aesthetic. The Upper Follifoot gritstone of which Harewood Bank was made, part of the great millstone grit shield covering the area, provided a beautiful and durable building stone for the taking on Lascelles's own land – and the transport, let alone the purchase, of stone was a major item of expenditure and potential delay in any country house construction of the time. The site was also ideally placed for communications, to receive all the multifarious building materials and furnishings needed for the completion of a great eighteenth-century mansion. A major northbound turnpike ran through Harewood village from Leeds, and to the east lay the Great North Road from London to York and Scotland, with coaching stops at Ferrybridge, Tadcaster and Wetherby. Tadcaster was also the river terminus for goods shipped in flat-bottomed boats along the Humber, Ouse and Wharfe from Hull, the country's chief port of entry for timber from Scandinavia and the principal northern port on the coastal route from London. From Hull to Tadcaster was a journey of a hundred miles, with another eleven by road to Harewood. On several occasions during the building of the house, the comparative costs of shipping via Hull or using horse-drawn road transport had to be studied, but the very existence of a choice was something not open to every aspiring stately home owner.

Lascelles's grand design began modestly enough in April 1755 with the building of a new stable block immediately to the west of the Old Hall, in which the Lascelles family continued to live until the 'New

House at Gawthorp', as it was known, became habitable in 1771. A
practical, hard-headed Yorkshireman with his father's business acu-
men, Lascelles was determined to conduct the building programme personally from the start. His friend Richard Sykes, another prosperous
landowner whose family had amassed a fortune as merchants in Leeds
and Hull, had decided to replace his own old-fashioned manor house at
Sledmere and intended to be his own architect, drawing on the skills and
knowledge of local master craftsmen. Lascelles wrote to him in April: 'I
. . . shall stand much in need of the experience & assistance of such
Adepts as you. The first step, I am told, is to provide the main materials;
and wood & Iron being of the number, I flatter myself I shall learn from
you, the Lowest price of the latter. . . .' Sykes's reply recommended
keeping ample timber and iron in stock in case war with France should
interfere with supplies, and he advised Lascelles to 'fortifie your self
with a Multitude of Patience'.

There is some confusion about the sequence of events in Lascelles's
eventual choice of architect. Clearly, the design of the stables would
have to be in keeping with that of the new house, and Lascelles's first
inclination seems to have been to commission Sir William Chambers,
then setting up his architectural practice in London at the age of
twenty-nine, and later to be the designer of Somerset House and Melbourne House in Piccadilly, which became the Albany apartment building. Chambers had just designed a triumphal arch for the entrance to
Inigo Jones's Wilton House in Somerset and would shortly undertake
the stable block at Goodwood House in Sussex. He submitted drawings
for the house at Harewood along with an elaborately rustic elevation
for the stables. Lascelles rejected both and chose instead John Carr of
York, whose father Robert was Lascelles's clerk of the works. Carr at
thirty-two already had a solid reputation locally as a mason and a building contractor as well as an architect of classical simplicity and elegance.
He produced a handsome, effective design for a low stable block surrounding a colonnaded courtyard with an arched entrance, and work
on the building began that same month, April 1755.

Lascelles used the progress of the stable block to acquire a practical
inside knowledge of building which he later applied effectively to the
construction of the house. He chose his craftsmen carefully, watched
their bills with an eagle eye and insisted on the best quality materials at
the most competitive prices. The local stone proved admirable to work,
though Lascelles complained that it cost as much as Portland, presum-

ably in labour charges. He got a skilled Harewood family of masons called Muschamp to submit a cut-price tender but even so complained to his steward that Muschamp made a shilling a day profit out of what he paid his workmen, adding pointedly: 'I don't doubt making a much better Bargain for my house.' The steward, Samuel Popplewell, now found himself with an unwelcome load of new responsibilities; one that was to burden him for years throughout the construction of Harewood House. He must have been a man of stoic patience, for besides charging him with supervising the workmen, the delivery of materials, building progress and wages, all on top of his regular duties of running the estate, Lascelles was constantly criticizing his steward's accounting and instructing him to be more efficient and economical. On one occasion he told Popplewell that every brick being fired on the estate should be counted and only the sound ones paid for – in one summer alone that involved checking 215,000 bricks.

The stable block was finished in good time, within three years, and Carr had meanwhile made some alterations to the Old Hall, despite the short lease of life remaining to it. Scaffolding went up on the site for the new house at the beginning of 1756, only to be blown down in February by galeforce winds. Even then, it seems, Lascelles had not finally decided on an architect. He wanted to 'improve his place', as the current phrase went, by an integrated plan that would encompass the house, the grounds and even the design of the village; this was accepted practice among a number of wealthy eighteenth-century landowners and contributed in a distinctive fashion to changing the face of England's countryside.

The prevailing architectural fashion for country houses at this time was an Anglicized version of the balanced classical style perfected by Andrea Palladio, but Lascelles felt this was a trifle conservative. His own tastes, surprisingly for a Yorkshire country gentleman, leaned towards French culture and fashion, and he liked French architecture as well as food: the housekeeper of his London home once warned the staff at Gawthorp to prepare their stomachs and palates for 'all frinsh [*sic*] Dishes, for we air all a Modaparre [*à la mode de Paris*].' William Chambers, who had spent his boyhood at Ripon, only twenty miles from Harewood, had gained his architectural training in Paris and had just returned from three years in Rome; his Yorkshire friend John Hall Stevenson of Skelton Hall thought his background fitted him ideally to gain the coveted Harewood commission and told him in November

1755 that he had prevailed upon Lascelles to consider a set of drawings by Chambers. 'I beg you will prepare a plan for a house of thirty thousand pounds for Mr Lascelles . . . he has had plans from Everybody in England. . . . This wd be a great stroke for you if you succeed. . . .'

Lascelles paid Chambers £100 for the drawings in June 1756 – cautiously, as ever, making sure he got a receipt – but the design, impressive enough with its large first-floor portico and pediment supported on Corinthian pillars and its graceful pavilions finishing off each wing, may have struck him as too academic; the interior plan certainly does not seem to have been a practical design for country living. One large room adjoining the wine cellars was labelled 'Empty Bottles'; another, in the south-west basement, 'For Flowers in Winter'; much space was wastefully disposed. Chambers also included a nursery suite adjoining Mrs Lascelles's dressing room; this would have had a sad irony for, although a son was born as the plans were being drawn up, both Lascelles children were to die in infancy.

In any event, Chambers's design was rejected, to his intense annoyance; when, ten years later, he used one of the end pavilions in his plan for the casino at Marino, near Dublin (generally reckoned one of his best small works) he noted with irritation that it had originally been part of 'a considerable composition . . . which among many others his Lordship procured for Harewood House.'

Capability Brown, whose early career included several essays into architecture before he settled down to concentrate on landscaping, also submitted two general plans for the house, probably in the Palladian mode he favoured, but these do not seem to have been seriously considered. In any case, John Carr's qualifications were plainly manifesting themselves in stone and mortar as the stable block arose, and Carr had advanced drawings for the house ready by February 1756. Lascelles evidently wanted some suggestions of his own incorporated, because Robert Carr wrote to say that the requirements would take some time to work out and it might be difficult to arrange a price. Carr junior was meanwhile carrying out other commissions for Lord Rockingham, one of Lascelles's Whig mentors, and for Lord Burlington, the pioneer patron of English Palladian architecture. He was also engaged in making extensive alterations to Daniel Lascelles's nearby country home at Plompton.

Time went on without the Harewood commission being settled, and then in June 1758 Lascelles was introduced by a friend to Robert Adam,

the Scottish architect, who like Chambers had just returned from studying in Italy and was establishing a practice in London. Impressed by his
ideas for a lighter, more domestic style of neoclassicism, Lascelles
showed him Carr's Palladian designs. Adam made some changes, bringing the portico forward, adding bold dressings round the windows and
changing the pavilion fronts. In a casual postscript to a letter to his
brother James in Edinburgh he wrote: 'I have thrown in Large Semi-
Circular Back Courts with columns betwixt the House and Wings.' His
brother replied: 'It affords me the greatest pleasure to think that you
have got Lascelles's plan improv'd to your mind, & that you have
tickled it up so as to dazzle the Eyes of the Squire.' He added that he
hoped it would satisfy the owner and earn Robert £700 for his advice.

But once again, Lascelles took his time about deciding. The semicircular courts were a drastic departure from Palladian style and he was
concerned that Carr might take it as an affront to his professional reputation. Adam and the lady who had introduced Lascelles to him were
annoyed and vowed that if they did not get a decision from him they
would 'never see his face again'. As Robert wrote to James in September
1758: '. . . if the Man likes it, It is very Cruel not to say so, & if he does
not why wou'd he keep one in Suspence [*sic*] or propose his Alterations,
or a new Plan.'

The answer was that Lascelles was unashamedly trying to achieve a
compromise out of both architects' skill which he felt would combine
the best of the old and newer styles of classical architecture. What in the
end he decided on, though there is no record of how he obtained both
men's consent, was to take Carr's practical, conservative plan for the
family apartments on the east side of the house and Adam's more
dramatic concept for a circuit of state apartments on the west, the two
arrangements divided by the main entrance hall and the saloon on a
north–south axis. In fact, Adam's semicircular court was removed from
the plan because of construction difficulties in 1762, only three years
after building began, and the west wing reverted to Carr's original
design. Responsibility for translating the amalgamated designs was
delegated to Carr and the long-suffering Samuel Popplewell, who began
to set out the lines at the end of 1758. On Twelfth Night, 1759, in
the depths of a hard Yorkshire winter, workmen began to dig out the
foundations.

3

The Making of an English Masterpiece

The first money that Edwin Lascelles laid out on his 'New House at Gawthorp' was modest enough – on 6 January 1759 the steward, Samuel Popplewell, paid John Wood and another labourer £2 13s. for 231 yards of digging in the frostbound earth. Twenty-three years later, when Lascelles, a notoriously slow payer where hired professionals were concerned (though not with artisans), finally settled his last account with Capability Brown, he had invested a total of £50,000 in the building, furnishing and landscaping of the house. It was £20,000 more than he originally anticipated and represented something like a million in the debased currency of our own day, although not for many millions could any ambitious man of taste today command such skills as those which created Lascelles's English masterpiece. They existed for a fleeting period in history and in the hands and brains of a very few men.

One of them, for whom Harewood House was to be the peak of his artistic achievement, an exquisitely dovetailed mosaic planned and executed as a unique whole, happened to be born only a couple of hours' leisurely ride from the site of his greatest triumph. In the early eighteenth century Otley was already a market town of great antiquity, with a history going back to the Roman occupation. Sheltered beneath the towering, craggy shoulder of Otley Chevin, it was the hub of commercial activity for all the farms and feudal estates in the area and the crafts associated with them. Here, in a house probably situated in Boroughgate, where the Otley Building Society today carries a bronze tablet in commemoration, Thomas Chippendale was born in 1718 to a joiner called John Chippindale, as he spelled it, and his wife Mary, the daughter of a stonemason. John's family for three generations before him had worked on the Farnley estate, felling wood, carpentering and working in other capacities for the Fawkes family, from surveying to making cart wheels, 'hewing and working up husbandry gear', repairing garden seats and farm gates.

The geographical closeness of Harewood and Otley encouraged a myth in later years that Edwin Lascelles had in some way 'discovered' Chippendale and was responsible for advancing his career, a view actively promoted in the 1920s by a Chippendale descendant. But nothing in the Harewood papers suggests the existence of such a relationship. On the contrary, says Chippendale's most recent biographer, Christopher Gilbert, they 'convey an impression that Edwin Lascelles was simply ordering furniture on Adam's advice from an elite London firm'. By the time Lascelles laid his foundation stone, on 23 March 1759, Chippendale had been for seven years the biggest name in English cabinet-making; his publication of *The Gentleman and Cabinet Maker's Director* in 1752 had been hailed as a landmark in furniture design.

Chippendale's early years have left a tantalizing gap between his baptism in Otley parish church and his marriage to Catherine Redshaw at St George's Chapel, Mayfair, on 19 May 1748. He probably worked for a while in York, which was the centre of fine craftsmanship for the region – and which contributed more than any other provincial city to the list of subscribers for the *Director*. In London, the newly married Chippendale lived first in Somerset Court off the Strand while preparing the *Director*, and then opened a workshop in three adjoining houses in upper St Martin's Lane, Nos 60 to 62. The street was an enclave of prosperous craftsmen living above their workshops – among Chippendale's neighbours was the well-known cabinetmaker William Vile – and the men used to congregate for refreshment at Slaughter's Coffee House, across the street from Chippendale's shop. His trade, despite a disastrous workshop fire in 1755, prospered and he became the first choice of the fastidious Robert Adam to furnish the rooms he was designing for houses up and down the country.

It was not until 1767, however, that Harewood was in a fit state to receive the professional attentions of England's leading cabinetmaker. The building of the stone mansion was a slow affair, made slower by the decision to demolish and remodel Adam's open inner court in 1762–65, and by John Carr's concurrent work on altering Goldsborough Hall, a large Jacobean manor ten miles away which Daniel Lascelles, now divorced, childless and wishing to live closer to his elder brother than Knaresborough, purchased in 1760.

But if the work was slow, it was of first-rate quality; Lascelles and his sharp-eyed steward saw to that. More than two hundred years later, as a historian of the house has noted, the bevelled edges of the 'rusticated' blocks of stone forming the basement storey are still as crisp as when John Muschamp and his team of a dozen local masons fitted them together. Stone had overtaken external brickwork in architectural fashion and Harewood's beautiful pale gritstone was hewn out of the quarries – still in existence, though long defunct – at the north end of the estate, most of it to be cut into large, square, smooth-fitting blocks or ashlar. Muschamp charged fivepence a foot for ashlar, of which there was to be 56,488 feet in the construction, and six shillings a foot for the dressed 'rustic' work, of which there would be 11,740 feet. His account eventually came to £4238 10s. 11d. The internal brickwork, laid by John Dodgson with bricks made of local clay, cost £680 10s. 10d. Carr was paid the meagre sum of £60 a year for his 'drawings and attendance', but there is no record of Adam's fee. After 1765, when his structural contribution was abandoned, Adam's role was restricted to the interior design, and in fact he did all his drawings for the rooms that year while Lascelles spent the summer travelling in Europe.

Cost and quality were controlled by the fact that nearly all the basic materials for the house came from local sources. Not only did the stone and bricks come from land owned by Lascelles, but even the plaster was made from gypsum dug out of pits on Lascelles land at Ribston. About a hundred tons were produced locally for the house, with additional fine-quality plaster coming from Roche Abbey in southern Yorkshire at two shillings or half a crown a ton. Ornamental plasterwork was an important part of any Adam ceiling and plasterers were skilled and versatile craftsmen, capable of decorative work as well as the more mundane tasks of laying flagstones and packing reeds for sound insulation into the joists of floors. Reeds, which cost sixpence a bundle, were regarded as superior to straw, which was sometimes thrust in underneath the floorboards with the ears still attached. Decorative plasterwork was charged at an astonishingly cheap rate of labour, only twopence a foot for a moulding of 'Carvd [sic] beads and Roaping', fourpence a foot for an ornamental cornice. The main work of plastering at Harewood was done by Thomas Rothwell, but for the principal rooms Adam called in his own stucco experts, Joseph Rose and Richard Mott.

The only material imported from outside the area in any quantity was wood. English oak being scarce, most of the wood for the structure, chiefly deal and fir, came from the Baltic via Hull. The famous mahogany doors were made of wood brought from the Lascelles estates in the West Indies, transported through Hull to Tadcaster and carefully seasoned by the Harewood joinery firm of Riley and Walker before being sawed into shape by another local partnership named Mawson and Senton. The timber buying was about the only aspect of procurement for which Lascelles used an agent, William Smith of Leeds; for almost everything else, he acted on his own behalf. The house eventually contained 362 doors and windows, and for the latter 4788 pounds of lead were brought from the mines at Grassington, thirty miles away, to make weights for the sash cords. Ironwork for the house came mainly from John Cockshutt's works at Wortley, though the elegant wrought iron of the main staircase is thought to have been executed by Maurice Tobin, a well-known 'whitesmith', or superior ironworker, of Leeds.

Majestically, the vast structure rose on the south slope of Harewood Bank. It had a large basement area, in the Georgian mode, with a pillared 'sub-hall' and huge cellars stretching underneath the carriage drive. Originally, the front entrance on the north side was approached by a flight of ten steps, but these were reduced in number when the level of the drive was raised during Sir Charles Barry's nineteenth-century alterations. Mary Mauchline, in her meticulously detailed account of the building, makes the interesting point that in those days spheres of work were not rigidly defined, making possible a kind of team effort which could not, one suspects, exist under trade unionism; though to be fair it could be argued that the system exploited some craftsmen.

> Each trade or craft made equipment and tools for others, building tradesmen undertook a share of work properly the task of more highly skilled and specialist craftsmen, who in turn ventured into the province of the decorative artists. . . . Contemporary building records list the master mason, bricklayer, carpenter and plumber along with the decorative craftsmen, drawing no distinction between the merits of their respective contributions to the creation of a house. . . .

Masons earned 1s. 8d. a day at the beginning of the 1770s and had to provide their own tools; apprentices and labourers about 1s. 2d.

In 1767, when Chippendale first came to Harewood, masons were still working in the rooms and the State Bedchamber, which was to contain some of his most elaborate and expensive pieces, was littered with lumps of stone. The famous cabinetmaker was engaged on furnishing Nostell Priory for Sir Rowland Winn when he accepted Lascelles's commission, and after his first visit to Harewood wrote to Winn: 'As soon as I had got to Mr Laselles [*sic*] and look'd over the whole of ye house I found that [I] Shou'd want a Many designs & Knowing that I had time Enough I went to York to do them.' These first designs would have been small, highly finished sketches of the type that Sir William Chambers, when Chippendale was furnishing Melbourne House in Piccadilly, complained were too small for a client to evaluate properly. Once approved by the client, the custom was for these small designs to be translated into large-scale technical drawings, and a group of such drawings exist in the Harewood archives. Unlike Chambers, Adam never seems to have complained about the smallness of Chippendale's first sketches.

On 20 October 1769 Chippendale's representative, Samuel James, arrived at Harewood to set the work in train. He spent a couple of days in Leeds ordering wallpaper, curtain fabric, serge, green baize and carpets, and then began work in the attic bedrooms, preparing canvas for the wallpaper backing and unpacking bedding. The rooms were named after the pattern of their curtain material; Red Stripe, Blue Stripe, Bamboo, Chintz. James's services were charged to Lascelles by Chippendale at the rate of four shillings a day; he worked at the house until just before Christmas 1769 and his successor, William Reid, arrived from London the following March. Chippendale, or rather his firm of Chippendale and Haig, offered a comprehensive service. Among Reid's functions were unpacking furniture, upholstering, laying carpets, hanging wallpaper, putting up Venetian blinds, making 'petty-coates' for the ladies' dressing-tables, cleaning furniture, restuffing mattresses and beating them to get rid of bugs. A contemporary authority on hygiene advised: 'All sorts of Beds, especially Feather-Beds, ought to be changed, driven or washed, at least three or four times a year; else it is impossible to keep them sweet and clean, and to prevent the Generation of Vermin'. Reid also made leather protective covers for the ornamental bedposts, oilcloth runners for the sideboards, sandbags to keep out draughts, a canvas backing for a large plan by Capability Brown and new hassocks for the church. Lining the plate closet with baize took him a fortnight; it is still very much in use to house the splendid collection of gold and silver dinner services accumulated by later generations of Lascelles.

Chippendale's charges for sending his trusted London workmen to Yorkshire included coach hire, travelling time, expenses on the road and lodging and half board – on top of a flat rate of £1 a week. In 1775 Reid's coach return fare to Yorkshire cost £3 13s. 6d. plus £1 4s. expenses, but the following year Lascelles was able to share the expense, as Reid was also working at Daniel Lascelles's home, Goldsborough Hall, and Sir William Weddell's Newby Hall. Some landowners were incensed by this practice of Chippendale's, claiming that they could have got local men to do the job just as well. Reid did have some local help – a gilder called Brown, a joiner called John Walker, a painter called Brewer and a carver from Doncaster called Theakstone. But in any event, Chippendale was on a losing wicket. In modern terms his problem was one of chronic cash-flow. Not only Lascelles but most of his other landed employers treated their 'tradesmen' with the cavalier attitude of Sir Edward Knatchbull of Mersham Le Hatch in Kent: 'As I receive my rents once a year, so I pay my Tradesmen's Bills once a year, wch is not reckoned very bad pay as ye world goes. . . .'

Men like Chippendale fell awkwardly in the commercial hierarchy between the professional man, like the architect, who only needed to issue a gentlemanly reminder of monies due, and the humble artisan, who was invariably paid on the nail. Yet Chippendale had to find the money to pay a workforce of forty or fifty men – an outlay of about £50 a week – and to settle with suppliers and subcontractors on a regular basis, or pay interest on their accounts. In 1772 he plaintively told Sir Rowland Winn: 'I have given bills to the amount of £4600 and they absolutly [sic] must be paid.' It is hard to escape the suspicion that wealthy employers like Lascelles relied on tradesmen like Chippendale being financially unable to resort to litigation; though Chippendale did once threaten legal action against the actor David Garrick, for whom he furnished houses in Royal Adelphi Street and Southampton Street, London, and a villa at Hampton on the Thames.

The only alternative to this cash blockage was to take on more and more work, which inevitably led to complaints that Chippendale was never able to get anything completed on time. 'I have been obliged,' Chippendale wrote to Sir Rowland Winn in 1770, 'to do business for ready Money Only in Order to Support My Self in ye best Manner I Could and that but very poorly.' (He had a large enough family to support: nine children by this time by his first wife Catherine, who died in 1772, with another three to come after he married Elizabeth Davis in 1777.)

During the eleven years he was engaged at Harewood, 1767 to 1778, Chippendale was working at full stretch on more than thirty other commissions up and down the country, from Berwickshire to Devon, and is thought to have visited the Lascelles house only twice, in September 1774 and February 1776. His work in Yorkshire alone during his Harewood years encompassed ten other great houses, including Nostell Priory, Temple Newsam House, Burton Constable Hall, Newby Hall, Denton Hall and Goldsborough Hall. In London his principal works were Lansdowne House in Berkeley Square, Melbourne House in Piccadilly (remodelled in 1804 into the Albany apartments) and Kenwood House on the leafy heights of Highgate. His patrons formed a cross-section of the landowning classes, from earls to merchant bankers, and an interesting family link occurred in 1775 between two of them when Sir Richard Worsley of Appuldurcombe House in the Isle of Wight, one of Chippendale's major commissions, married Seymour Dorothy Fleming, a stepdaughter of Edwin Lascelles by his second marriage to Lady Jane Fleming.

Edwin Lascelles's bills with Chippendale reached shameful heights even for a section of society which habitually regarded its tradesmen as a form of interest-free credit – an attitude that persisted until well after the Second World War. After five years' work at Harewood, Chippendale's firm was owed more than £3000; four years later it was £6838. During all this time Lascelles had paid only small sums on account, none larger than £25. At one point Chippendale actually went on strike, refusing to do any more work at Harewood until he was paid, and even the loyal Popplewell was moved to write to his master: 'I do not wonder at Chippendale's Stoping, if he had so much owing as he said he had.'

Chippendale's employers may have grumbled about the cost of his workmen, but they put in punishing hours. Reid regularly worked a six-day, seventy-two-hour week, working in all about a thousand hours between 1771 and 1776 and receiving Popplewell's accolade of being 'very diligent'. They may also have cavilled at his charges for packing and transporting his best pieces, made in the London workshop, but later generations would be grateful for the care with which Chippendale dispatched his creations by the ill-sprung wagons of the time. To transport 'richly finished' chairs, for instance, he required 'a close case of full half-inch deal,' in which the chairs, carefully wrapped in paper, were freely suspended from cross battens by screws driven into the undersides of the rails, thus avoiding friction with the sides of the crate. Screw holes can be found underneath the seat rails of many Chippendale chairs and are regarded as one voucher of authenticity.

It was up to the client to choose his method of transport – road, canal or coastal vessel – and to pay the freight charges, which were not cheap. Six fine cabriole armchairs, a large pier glass, a fine secretaire and commode, all made for the State Bedchamber, were sent by road to Harewood from London for £42 9s. 4d., the wood, battens and protective matting for the packing cases being charged extra at £9 5s. Most of the consignments to Harewood, beginning in April 1769, were conveyed by the regular London–Leeds carriers Green, Jackson and Fisher, whose wagons loaded at the White Horse, Cripplegate, and who charged a standard rate of £7 6s. 8d. a ton.

Chippendale's work for Harewood, despite the loss of those pieces which death duties or other exigencies have forced the family to sell, remains a virtuoso display of craftsmanship. It ranges from the purely decorative, like the eight delicate carved and painted beechwood chairs in the entrance hall which deliberately echo Joseph Rose's plasterwork rondels in the ceiling, to pieces which, while lacking nothing in beauty and ornament, were designed to fulfil a practical function. Perhaps the most striking example of these is the magnificent set of urns flanking a matching sideboard in the Dining Room; the upper portion of the urns, lead lined, served as a wine cooler, while the lower part was a silver chest. The set is often described as among the most superb furniture ever made in England, and the wine coolers were still being put to practical use for state banquets in the late 1950s.

The State Bedchamber on the ground floor was fitted out in particularly lavish style with carved and gilded furniture, and was the wonder of the first visitors to Harewood House in the 1790s. Its chief glory was what Chippendale in his accounts described as

> a very large State Bedstead with a Dome Canopy decorated in the Inside with rich Carved Antique Ornaments – a large Antique Vauze on the Top, with Corner vases and sundry other Ornaments, the Cornishes with Emblematic Tablets and Swags of Roses, with various other ornaments exceeding richly Carved, the Posts fluted and very richly Carved – the whole Gilt in Burnished Gold, exceedingly highly finished – large Castors &c. £250.

Chippendale added a further £150 for making up the rich green and yellow silk damask hangings; Lascelles supplied the damask but Chippendale's man Reid bought the silk lining, tassels and other trimmings.

Chippendale was in the habit of equipping his best beds with layer on layer of mattresses, reminiscent of the princess and the pea; feather upon flock upon a thick bottom mattress of hair. For the Harewood state bed this cost another £50 odd including blankets, counterpanes and down pillows (but not sheets). Fourteen guineas of that went on a 'fine large Bordered Bed Tick and Bolster filled with the finest and best seasoned Hudsons Bay Feathers' (they were twice the price of mere 'Dantzic feathers'). When not in use, the bed was sheathed in protective covers of paper and canvas specially tailored by Reid. The walls of the bedchamber were hung with matching green silk damask and the curtains were of green and yellow damask under gilded cornices which cost £26 the pair. Chippendale's accounts for this room covered every detail from sewing silk for the wall hangings (£9 10s.) to twelve brass screw pulleys at a shilling each. When Sir Charles Barry remodelled the house in the 1840s, the State Bedchamber became a sitting room (as the Princess Royal's sitting room, it was one of the last three rooms to be opened to the public in 1966), and the grandly voluptuous bed was dismantled and stored until it was recently removed for restoration, still with the remnants of its original damask.

The lavishness of Chippendale's original concept extended to both the lady's and gentleman's dressing rooms, the latter being graced with a carved pier glass at a cost of £360 – £290 for the glass, which then carried a heavy tax, and £70 for the 'exceeding richly Carved' frame. It also had the famous 'Diana and Minerva' commode, 'curiously inlaid and Engraved', which is today in the Princess Royal's sitting room and a celebrated feature of Harewood's furnishings. It cost originally £86.

In the master bedroom suite, as elsewhere in the house, Chippendale demonstrated his mastery of a range of cabinet finishes from lacquer to ivory inlay to marquetry, and of styles from Adam's neoclassicism to rococo and the chinoiserie which was just becoming fashionable. His hand even extended to the design and printing of special wallpaper for the Gallery – a pattern of palms and 'antique ornament' on a pink ground, for which he charged three guineas for making the drawings and thirty shillings for each of the forty-one pieces of wallpaper. Unique in his whole *oeuvre* are the carved and painted trompe l'oeil pelmets in the Gallery, which still easily deceive the eye of today's visitors, having been restored to imitate heavy dark blue, gilt-fringed taffeta.

Chippendale's son Thomas contributed some pieces to Harewood, notably the semicircular console tables decorated with goats' heads in the Gallery, and there has long been controversy among scholars over whether Chippendale subcontracted some of his best-known pieces. If so, says his biographer Christopher Gilbert, the most likely area was in marquetry; it suddenly became fashionable in the early 1770s and it might have been difficult for Chippendale to assemble a team of highly skilled marquetry workers at short notice. But Gilbert is certain that Chippendale retained overall control of design and execution. As to the designs themselves, the one-time theory of a partnership between Robert Adam and Chippendale is now exploded, the only authenticated Adam pieces at Harewood today being a pair of pedestals in the private Inner Hall leading to the main staircase.

That Adam dominated his team of craftsmen, however, is not in doubt. Harewood was the first of his great country houses to which he would bring his team of hand-picked artist-craftsmen; one London client remarked on his 'regiment of artificers', from bricklayers to decorative painters. He certainly provided sketches for Chippendale along with his other contractors, though Edwin Lascelles in turn steered Adam firmly in the direction he wanted to go. Adam planned most of the major rooms – Library, Music Room, Gallery, State Bedchamber, Saloon, Dining Room, owner's suite of study, bedroom and dressing room, Entrance Hall, Staircase and the Circular Room, which was originally an elaborately decorated dressing-room for Lascelles and disappeared in the Victorian remodelling. Adam also designed the friezes for the main apartments and most of the ceilings and chimneypieces. The Gallery, with its seven unique mirrors – among the largest in England – reflecting the light from seven tall windows, was the last room to be completed, in 1780. It occupied the entire west wing, measured 77 feet long by 24 feet wide, and Adam intended it to be the crowning glory of his interior design. John Jewell, the Harewood House porter who wrote a guidebook in his spare time, described it in 1819 as 'a show of magnificence and art such as the eye hath seldom seen'.

Among the artist-craftsmen Adam brought in his train was Joseph Rose, the stuccoist, who executed most of the fine ceilings and alone among Adam's collaborators was accustomed to be paid by the architect direct instead of having his bills approved by Adam and forwarded to the client for settlement. Rose, like most of Adam's decorators, worked with him on other commissions – Nostell, Syon and

Kenwood among them. He is also credited with the entire building of
Sledmere, the Sykes family home in the East Riding.

Two other noted Adam recruits were Angelica Kauffmann, the
Swiss-born decorator who had taken London by storm as a young artist
of twenty-five in 1766, created a gossip-column reputation as a society
flirt and became one of two women founder members of the Royal
Academy; and Antonio Zucchi, who became her second husband in
1781. Kauffmann, whose decorative murals can be seen in the Gallery,
the Old Library and other rooms, along with the spectacular Music
Room ceiling, enjoyed a *succès d'estime* among the English artistic
establishment – with the notable exception of the portrait painter
John Hoppner, who believed that she had corrupted the public taste
in painting. Joseph Farington, the art connoisseur and diarist,
calculated that she earned about £14,000 during her time in England
and that Zucchi, who married her when he was about seventy
and who worked with her on several great Adam houses, made about
£8000.

In the midst of all this furnishing and decorating, Edwin Lascelles
married for the second time, and when the couple moved in 1771 into
the new house, along with Lady Jane's two daughters, inevitable
changes were required. But on the whole the house offered a comfortable and practical design for living: its sanitation arrangements, if not as
advanced as the latest innovations in the field, allowed several water
closets, including one connected by a carpeted passage to a suite of
family rooms, and also a hot bath in the basement, beneath the Dining
Room. The Library, though well designed for its purpose, seems at first
to have been a poor relation of Lascelles's well-equipped London
library – an early visitor commented superciliously that it contained
only 'a few Pamphlets, some old Newspapers and a defence of Mr Pitts
Conduct on the Regency Affair' – but a century later another writer
praised its fine, large collection of books as a refreshing change from
most country-house libraries which were 'full of all kinds of treasures
except the bibliographical'. The family spent most of its time in the
Yellow Damask Room next to the Saloon, where the upholstery and
wall hangings were both of that material (it is now named the Rose
Drawing Room and has undergone an appropriate change of decoration), and in the Coffee Room in the basement. The latter was an elegant
place to relax, graced by a set of satinwood chairs upholstered in needlework, and the adjoining Billiard Room was a favourite retreat of

Edwin Lascelles, with its billiard table by Gillow and its comfortable club armchairs in mahogany and red leather.

There were the usual teething troubles of any new house: ventilators had to be installed in the kitchens to 'take away the disagreeable smells'; a housemaid forgot to remove the boards closing off the chimney in the library before lighting the fire, with the result that smoke billowed out, blackening everything in the room including Joseph Rose's fine new stucco work and the ceiling in Lascelles's adjoining dressing room. Lascelles remained calm about the mishap; the rooms were cleaned by washing and sponging until 'the nicest Eye cannot discern it', and the distraught housemaid was reassured by her employer, who said she was a good worker and all the other chimney boards should be burned to prevent a similar mistake.

There remained one major enterprise to set in train – the landscaping of the grounds. In 1772, when Old Gawthorp Hall had finally been demolished, the most famous landscape designer in England paid his first visit to Harewood. Capability Brown was fifty-six, with twenty years' experience of landscaping and a list of distinguished commissions behind him. He had laid out the grounds for some of the greatest country houses in England including Longleat, Luton Hoo, Blenheim, Ragley Hall, Bowood, Castle Ashby, Holkham and Chatsworth. The architect James Paine, who was responsible for contemporary additions to Chatsworth, remarked that Brown's talents had contributed towards making the Duke of Devonshire's seat 'perhaps one of the noblest places in Europe'.

Born in Northumberland, Brown had early architectural ambitions and in fact designed some rather fine houses (his fellow landscapist Humphry Repton praised them as 'second to none), including Claremont in Surrey for Clive of India, Croome Park in Worcestershire for the sixth Earl of Coventry, additions to Burghley for the Earl of Exeter, considerable extensions to Lord Palmerston's Hampshire home Broadlands (later to pass to Lord Louis Mountbatten through his wife's Cassel banking family), and the Marquess of Bute's Cardiff Castle. His formative work on landscape had been with William Kent on laying out the grounds at Stowe, then Lord Cobham's private estate and now the public school, between 1740 and 1750; it was late in the 1740s that Brown obtained his first landscape commission, advising Lord Brooke about the grounds of Warwick Castle.

A somewhat lugubrious-looking man, to judge from his portrait by

Sir Nathaniel Dance, with a long, heavy nose, astute eyes and a hint of cynical amusement about the mouth, Brown gained his undying nickname not so much from his own abilities, as from his habit of remarking on the 'capability' of this or that site. Brown's special contribution to landscape design – indeed, to the face of England itself – was to introduce a studied naturalness, to work with the grain of nature, making the minimum of changes; in his own analogy, to punctuate the existing landscape with a comma here, a colon there, a parenthesis or full stop somewhere else.

By the time he was thirty-three, he had won the reputation, in the words of Lord Chatham, of sharing 'the private hours of the King', of dining familiarly with the Duke of Northumberland and of sitting down 'at the tables of all the House of Lords'. Certainly he had no shortage of aristocratic clients, and his own capabilities were becoming legendary. A French contemporary said of 'Le Brun' that after riding round a property for an hour he would conceive the design for a whole park, and that half a day was sufficient for him to mark it all out on the ground. In 1764 he was appointed Surveyor to His Majesty's Gardens and Waters at Hampton Court, a post which brought him £2000 a year and a handsome seventeenth-century residence near the park called Wilderness House, a considerable step up from his first London home in Hammersmith.

Brown went to 'Gawthorpe', as he called the Lascelles mansion, three times during 1772. He quickly perceived the natural possibilities of the site with its stream which could be dammed to form a lake and its well-wooded contours which came into their full glory with the rich colours of autumn. During the next ten years – when Brown, like Chippendale, would be plagued by Lascelles's indolence in settling bills – he was engaged on a number of other commissions, both as landscape designer and architect. He designed Claremont, converted the ruins of Cardiff Castle into a habitable home for the Marquesses of Bute, landscaped the Backs at Cambridge, the grounds of Syon Park and the gardens at Cliveden, and made additions to Chilham Castle near Canterbury.

He encountered difficulties early on at Harewood. His first step in making the lake, on the site of the Old Hall, was to dam the Stank Beck and fill in the old canal, but once made, the lake persisted in leaking. As late as 1778, the indefatigable Popplewell recorded that there was still a hole in its bed 'large enough to bury a horse in'. Brown was unable to solve the problem and Lascelles had to call in someone else, a surveyor named John Hudson, who guaranteed his work for twenty-one years from 1780, for a fee of £1000.

Brown's first account, for making the lake and its islands and planting the encircling slopes, came to £900. Lascelles delayed settlement with the explanation: 'I have always said and did insist upon it that the ground was Scandalous lay'd and beggarly sown, and that Several other parts were Slovenly Run over and badly finished.' Another two years passed before he paid Brown any money – £600 in two instalments – and that was not until Brown had called upon him personally at his London residence to beg for payment. In May 1781 Lascelles finally settled the whole account, but running battles continued between Popplewell and those employees of Brown's who remained at Harewood to supervise the landscaping. Brown's bill eventually came to about £16,000 – three times the original estimate, and without the cost of planting – but for this sum, as a nineteenth-century writer enthused, 'one of the most beautiful domains in the kingdom was decorated'. The house, though not the largest, was 'as completely furnished and fitted up as any in the kingdom', he wrote. 'Nothing can exceed the work of the carver and the mason and the upholsterer, everything being in the most costly and best taste . . . though the prospect is not very extensive, the rising brow in front of the house, with its plantations, buildings and the water beneath it, afford a very pleasing view. . . .' Much of the effectiveness of Harewood, he concluded, 'results from its having been built and completed as a whole upon a settled and majestic plan, by a full purse, and with the avowed intention of making it one of the finest houses in England.'

Lascelles may have professed dissatisfaction with some of Brown's work but it is noteworthy that early visitors to Harewood, newly embowered in its 1800-acre park, invariably singled out the setting for praise. The Lichfield poet Anna Seward was more impressed by the grounds than by the house and the 'artificial splendour' of its seventeen state rooms. In 1813, a local historian of Wharfedale commented: 'There is nothing so interesting in the rich seat of the Earl of Harewood as its landscape garden, as Nature herself seems to have afforded the plan of improvement, demanding only her hills and dales, her woods and lakes, to be characterized and displayed to advantage . . . the gay, shining villa seated on a summit with circling trees, the spacious lake . . . the bright gardens; the verdant lawns and distant buildings . . . the background consisting of the hills of Wharfedale, Almscliffe, Fox Crag, etc. . . .' And a local poet named Maude rhapsodized: 'in yonder field near Harewood's splendid home, Where pleasure dwells and freedom feels at home.'

On 6 February 1783, a year after his Harewood bills were finally settled, Brown was taken ill suddenly and collapsed on returning home from a professional call on Lord Coventry in Piccadilly. A lifelong sufferer from asthma, he apparently fell down in a fit and died almost immediately, about 9 p.m. that evening. He was sixty-seven years old and his invention – or re-invention – of improving on nature had permanently changed the perception of the English towards their domestic landscape. Sir Robert Walpole noted in his diary: 'So closely did he copy nature that his works will be mistaken.' The Duke of Leinster once offered him a thousand pounds, payable on landing, if he would take his skills to Ireland, but Brown turned it down, saying he had 'not yet finished England'.

The Lascelles were now well ensconced in their country home, although for a full six years after taking possession work was still going on around them, with Chippendale's men hanging curtains and wallpaper, repairing troublesome Venetian blinds, fixing mirrors and other fitments, lining card-tables, laying carpets and 'taking the Feathers out of Beds & drying & beating them'. The house was already famed far beyond Yorkshire; three years after it was built Josiah Wedgwood featured its likeness on an ice-pail made for Catherine the Great. Lascelles divided his time between Harewood and his London home in Portman Street; a keen and knowledgeable gardener, he had made sure that Capability Brown's instructions included provision of a kitchen garden to supply his town house in season with fresh peaches, pineapples, strawberries, melons and french beans (a custom kept up to this day with regular dispatches from Leeds via British Rail's Red Star express service). The family would arrive in Yorkshire in early June, as soon as Parliament had recessed for the summer and the London season ended – earlier then than now – and often stayed until Christmas. Daniel Lascelles, though living so close, was always sure of a room if he wanted it.

Edwin Lascelles, who had been made Baron Harewood in 1790, died at Harewood House on Sunday, 25 March 1795. He was eighty-two and although he had no direct heir, he had founded one of the great country-house dynasties of England. The barony lapsed with his death and the estates passed to his cousin, Lieutenant-Colonel Edward Lascelles, the Tory MP for Northallerton. In June 1795 the diarist Joseph Farington noted the gossip current in London that the new master of Harewood House had been left £200,000 in assets and £50,000 a year, at least half of that coming from the family's West Indies interests. It was the equal of a duke's income and would transform the life of this unassuming Yorkshire squire with unusually cultivated tastes.

4

'Great Oaks that Shade
a Country'

Edward Lascelles was fifty-five, a former colonel of cavalry who had
served in the Seven Years' War and a popular figure in Harewood, when
he moved out of his own country seat, neighbouring Stapleton Park,
into his cousin's 'noble mansion . . . deservedly ranked with the finest
buildings in the kingdom', as the *Gentleman's Magazine* obituary
notice of Edwin Lascelles extolled it. Contemporary prints show the
house gracefully embowered on three sides by the woods planted by
Capability Brown and his men, the grassy park flowing up to the very
walls of the south front, which commanded a view over a serpentine
lake of thirty-two acres and beyond, countryside of 'the most beautiful
and picturesque scenes imaginable', as a guidebook described it a few
years later. On the north side of the house, Adam's splendid portico was
flanked by wings enriched with carved medallions representing Liberty,
Britannia, Agriculture and Commerce. From the top of the flight of
steps, guarded by two sphinxes, could be seen a sweeping panorama; to
the left, through a specially designed opening in the pleasure grounds,
Almscliffe Crag reared its bulk four miles away across the valley of the
Wharfe; to the right, another opening revealed what the guidebook
called 'a rich treat of scenery', pointed up in the foreground by
Harewood parish church, covered with ivy at its western end to the top
of the steeple. Above the north front steps was a large flagstoned terrace,
ornamented with eight lamps, beneath which were the coal stores for
the house. It was, the guidebook noted, 'a most complete and useful
family residence'. Edward Lascelles and his heir Edward 'Beau' Lascelles, the eldest of his ten children, were soon to make it more than that.
Far more than Edwin, the thrifty and practical builder of the house, his
cousin was a keen connoisseur of the arts who loved and was willing to

spend money on music, the theatre and collecting. His son shared his tastes, and under their influence Harewood House began to blossom with paintings and fine porcelain and to acquire the reputation it has continued to enjoy as a centre of cultural patronage in the north of England.

Colonel Lascelles did not long languish as a commoner. The barony of Harewood which had died with Edwin Lascelles for lack of a direct heir was – perhaps as the result of some discreet lobbying – revived in the summer of 1796 for the new incumbent of Harewood House, and he lost no time in having the firm of Chippendale and Haig decorate his hall chairs with the family crest and coronet. Edward took his seat in the House of Lords in March 1797, spending about twenty pounds on various 'introduction fees', the attendance charge for Garter King of Arms and a clerk to declaim the letters patent, as well as other disbursements expected of a new peer such as the ten shillings and sixpence 'to the Door Porter at the House of Lords' recorded in his account books. In 1812 he would be created first Earl of Harewood, establishing the dynasty that continues to flourish seven generations on.

By entering the aristocracy, Edward Lascelles entered a kingdom of influence and respect unimaginable to the peerage of today. There might be, as Lord Melbourne is reputed to have said of the Order of the Garter, 'no damned merit in it', but in the 1800s the landed aristocracy, even more than the landed gentry, ruled and were seen to rule, and no one effectively disputed Edmund Burke's dictum that they were the 'great oaks that shade a country, and perpetuate your benefits from generation to generation'. In eighteenth-century Parliaments, about two-thirds of the Commons were landowners, and the wealth represented by cultivated land in 1815, at an average capital value of £24 per acre, was about £750 million. The level of estate revenue had risen by 40 or 50 per cent between 1760 and 1790, though rents in some areas were deliberately kept low for political reasons, or to compensate tenants whose land was used for hunting over, or because the region was remote from markets. Land tax, originally introduced in the seventeenth century, was assessed on rents at 4s. in the pound in war years, but at other times was levied inequitably in different parts of the country, with certain areas, particularly the north and west, enjoying a political bias: a landowner in Kent or Essex might pay 4s. in the pound, but in Yorkshire it would be only 1s. 3d., and in Cornwall, Cumberland or Wales, a mere ninepence.

Edward Lascelles was not a rich man when he inherited his cousin's estate: his bankbooks, which had recorded credit balances of less than £200, were showing levels of £10,000 within two years of his change in status, though his outgoings were formidable too, and he was lucky if he ended the year with a thousand in hand. On taking over Harewood House he meticulously recorded finding £22 1s. in Lord Harewood's bureau, and when Popplewell the steward handed him £250 from various monies due to the estate, it must have come as a windfall. Yet he already spent quite lavishly for a country squire on books, music and plays. During 1790, for example, his account books showed entries of £18 4s. for music, five guineas for 'Plays and Operas' and a further £2 10s. 'to Two Plays', along with such mundane expenditures as £16 9s. for the services of a plumber, twelve shillings for 'Destroying Bugs in June 1789', and £2 3s. to Joseph Bramah, inventor of the famous security locks, for repairing his water closet. He was a ready subscriber to histories and other scholarly works brought out in instalments and in 1795, the year of his inheritance, an entry in his accounts read: 'To Jn White musician on acct £10 N.B. I promised to give him £50 a year.' (White became leader of a private orchestra at Harewood House.)

His apotheosis as Lord Harewood enabled him to expand his cultural interests, especially in late Georgian London, which at its fashionable hub around Mayfair and Piccadilly was a companionable village of gentlemanly dabblers in the arts. There were exhibitions at the Royal Academy (then in Somerset House) of contemporary artists like Turner, Reynolds and Hoppner, all of whom are well represented in Harewood House, and the portrait fees charged by these masters were a constant topic of conversation among fellow painters and potential sitters. According to the gossipy diaries of the minor Royal Academician Joseph Farington, Reynolds charged thirty-five guineas for a three-quarter-length portrait, Hoppner twenty-five guineas. Lawrence charged forty guineas for a three-quarter but wondered whether he should reduce his fee to match that of Reynolds. William Blake was beginning to be talked about as a designer and engraver of genius, though Hoppner remarked acidly that some of his designs 'were like the conceits of a drunken fellow or madman'. In the 1790s a ticket to Drury Lane for the season (about eighty performances) cost six guineas for any part of the house. Mrs Siddons could be seen as Lady Macbeth; Joseph Haydn was in London and attending soirees in fashionable houses where his songs were performed. The cultivated oligarchy patronized the picture galleries; Farington recorded that Gainsborough's pictures 'sold low'; *The Blue Boy*, which was to cause a furore in 1921 when the dealer Joseph Duveen engineered its sale to the American millionaire Henry Huntington for £148,000, went for only thirty-five guineas at Nuttals' saleroom in 1796. Some patrons badly misjudged the market; Warren Hastings gave a thousand guineas for a portrait of an Indian Nabob which was later sold at Christie's for seven guineas. Thomas Agnew's, the Bond Street dealers, were already noted for their annual exhibition of watercolour drawings and Edwin Lascelles's new house at Harewood gained immediate renown among the London cognoscenti when a picture of it by Girtin appeared there in November 1795.

The new Lord Harewood was also the subject of London gossip. Farington, who loved digging out information about other people's money, recorded on 14 November 1795: 'Hoppner has been at Mr Lascelles at Harewood House in Yorkshire. . . . Lord Harewood has left Mr. Lascelles £30,000 a year and £200,000 in money. Hoppner says they are very good people. He went with young Mr. Lascelles, who has a taste for the arts & has practised a little, several excursions to see remarkable places. Bolton Bridge is a very picturesque spot. . . .' A couple of months later, Farington was noting: 'Young Mr. Lascelles is reckoned very like the Prince of Wales. The Prince is not pleased at it. He calls Lascelles the Pretender. . . . At Brighton the Prince has been struck on the shoulder familiarly with "Ha Lascelles, how is it?" To which He has returned a marked look of disapprobation.' According to Farington, the Prince on one occasion ordered Hoppner to alter a portrait of him, complaining, 'It is more like the Pretender.'

With £30,000 a year, if Farington is to be believed, the new Lord Harewood was well placed to enjoy the luxuries of late Georgian life. In 1808, indeed, his income was officially assessed at £46,284; £30,345 of it from his landed estates. (This compared handsomely with the £57,000 drawn by the Duke of Marlborough, one of England's grandest landowners.) He could afford the essential status symbols of his new position, the London season and the great country house, for which the basic minimum requirement was reckoned to be £5000–£6000 a year. Immediately on his change of fortune, in 1795, he bought Roxburghe House in Hanover Square from the Duke of Roxburghe, a fine three-storeyed Adam mansion on the north side of the square. This also became known as Harewood House, and cost the new earl almost as much to maintain for the two to three months his family was in residence as the Yorkshire establishment did for the rest of the year. Prices being as stable as they then were, there is comparatively little difference in the accounts kept by the first earl and by his second son, who inherited in 1820 after Beau Lascelles's early death: in the 1800s it cost between £7000 and £9000 a year to run the two establishments and, in the 1820s and 1830s, about £10,000. Details of the family comings and goings were faithfully recorded by the house steward at Harewood in the cellar book, for the wines and spirits in stock had to be strictly accounted for. Most years, they would leave for London at the end of February – the servants going down six weeks beforehand to prepare everything – returning at the end of June, though it might vary by a month either way. Lord Harewood maintained a large household of servants, equal to some of the grandest dukes, with about fifty on his payroll in Yorkshire, most of whom would move to London for the season. The servants were paid twice a year, in May and November, the half-yearly wages ranging from £60 for the house steward down to £4 or £5 for a humble laundry maid. In 1821, the second Earl paid £1640 a year for his fifty servants, but some noble households ran to twice that: in 1825 two Yorkshire aristocrats, the Earl of Darlington and Earl Fitzwilliam, both spent more than £3000 on their domestic establishments and a staff of a hundred servants was not uncommon. The Reform Bill of 1832 caused some sharp retrenchment, when the aristocracy deemed it wiser for a time to adopt a more modest style of living, and households shrank further – and permanently – when the railways made coach travel redundant and with it the whole panoply of postilions, coachmen and ostlers.

In the eighteenth century the lower ranks of servants such as footmen, grooms, kitchen-maids and laundry-maids were recruited from the children of estate tenants and labourers; the higher-ranking, such as house steward, butler, cook, housekeeper and lady's maid, would be drawn from the families of local minor gentry, farmers and professional men. A yearly wage of £100 to £120 was usual for a house steward – a sort of glorified majordomo who looked after the cellar stock and the running of the domestic base; a head cook would receive about £40 and a housekeeper £20; a footman £8 and a maid £4 or £5. Lascelles' scale of pay at the beginning of the nineteenth century was quite generous. All would have free board and liveries where appropriate, and might pick up tips from house guests, depending on whether tipping was encouraged or not in that household. Food was ample and good; there was usually a plentiful supply of cold meat for the carving, tea and sometimes punch laced with rum or brandy, or a barrel of beer. When the head of a noble household died, his servants were issued with mourning clothes or the money to buy them; on the death of the first Earl of Harewood in 1820, mourning for the menservants alone cost £386 10s., and when the second Earl died in 1841 the lower-paid maids at Harewood House received a mourning grant amounting to about a third of their entire yearly wage.

A glance through the account books kept in London by the first and second earls gives an intimate glimpse of the day-to-day running of a fashionable Mayfair household. Many of the tradesmen's names are still part of London's commercial life, or were until recent times. Lord Harewood bought his groceries from Fortnum and Mason (sometimes listed as 'Mr. Fortnum'), his coal from Findlater's, his drugs from John Bell (not yet John Bell and Croyden), his soda water from J. Schweppe and Co. of Berners Street, his snuff from Mr. Fribourg, his silver from Rundell and Bridge, his hats from Lock's, his boots from Hoby's, his newspapers from Mudie's, his books from Hatchard of Piccadilly and his confectionery from Gunter's, a celebrated Mayfair pastry shop and ice-cream maker which only went out of business in the 1950s. The Harewoods were sociable in both generations, attending balls and taking boxes at the theatre and the opera. Horses were kept at livery during the season at John Tollit's livery stables, 157 Oxford Street, near the junction with Bond Street. An immense variety of household goods was required to run two establishments of this size, 200 miles apart, most of them eloquently redolent of the labour-intensive character of the times: quantities of 'best blacking', soft soap, yellow soap, linseed, starch, candles, whiting, ashes, lemons, rough salt, twine and edging for repairing carpets and a hundred other items requiring the application of work-roughened hands to floors, furniture, draperies, bed linen, fire grates and kitchen utensils.

The earl kept a well-stocked cellar at his Yorkshire seat, with port and sherry the most heavily represented. In 1805, the steward noted in his cellar book that when the family returned from London on 10 July, the cellar contained 2172 bottles of port, 2425 bottles of sherry, 941 of madeira, 226 of cane spirits, 163 of rum, 100 of claret, 129 of malmsey, 141 of sercial, 301 of hock and much lesser amounts of burgundy (twenty-three bottles) and champagne (one bottle of 'red champagne' and three of white). Most weeks would see a daily consumption of two bottles of port, one or two of madeira and one of sherry, with the odd bottle of hock or claret. Even the nursery received an occasional bottle of port – whether for the children or the nurse is not clear. At intervals a pipe of port or madeira would be bottled (624 bottles) to replenish the stock. Generous amounts of port, sherry, brandy and rum also went down to the servants' hall at Christmas.

But for the conscientious landowner, it was no idle responsibility running an estate the size of Harewood, and the Earls of Harewood early established a reputation as good land managers. In 1775 Nathaniel Kent published his *Hints to Gentlemen of Landed Property*, in which he advised: 'A Competent knowledge of Agriculture is the most useful science a gentleman can obtain; it is the noblest amusement the mind can employ itself in, and tends, at the same time, to the increase of private property and public benefit. . . . The gentleman's purse, and the farmer's labour, will do great things, when the contract between them is so contrived as to yield them mutual benefit.' But a gentleman could not be expected to master all the myriad skills needed to administer an estate, which was a full-time and well-paid occupation, although the famous Coke of Norfolk, having fired his agent for corruption, did the work himself between 7 a.m. and 10 a.m. each day, and some other 'improving landlords', notably the Duke of Bedford and the Duke of Bridgewater (who was a qualified engineer) insisted on being personally involved in the agent's work. It was generally reckoned that an estate had to produce more than £6000 a year in rents before it was worth employing a full-time agent, but for such estates the land agent or estate manager was a key figure in their prosperity. On him devolved not only the management of land and repair of walls, fences and drainage, but the selection of tenant farmers and the efficient collection of rents. He needed to be a man of many parts to earn the £800 a year he was paid at Harewood – some agents earned as much as £1000 a year in the nineteenth century. John Lockhart Morton, in a manual of estate management published in 1858, suggested that the thoroughly qualified farmer – which the agent had to be – should have more than a passing acquaintance with geology, chemistry, animal and vegetable physiology, zoology and veterinary surgery, as well as some knowledge of hydraulics and hydrostatics, meteorology and pneumatics. An estate manager, he opined, 'may exert an influence on agricultural progress of

The makers of Harewood and its collections

Edwin Lascelles,
Lord Harewood
(1712–95)

Edward Lascelles,
*1st Earl of
Harewood*
(1740–1820)

m. 1761, Anne,
daughter of
William Chaloner
of Guisborough

Edward,
Viscount Lascelles
(1764–1814)

Henry Lascelles,
*2nd Earl of
Harewood*
(1767–1841)

m. 1794, Henrietta,
daughter of
Sir John Sebright Bt

George Canning
(1770–1827)

Henry Lascelles,
*3rd Earl of
Harewood*
(1797–1857)

m. 1823, Lady
Louisa Thynne,
daughter of the
2nd Marquess
of Bath

Ulick de Burgh,
*14th Earl and
1st Marquess of
Clanricarde* KP, PC
(1802–74)

m. 1825,
Hon. Harriet
Canning
(1804–76)

Charles, *Earl
Canning* KG
(1812–62),
m. 1835, Hon.
Charlotte Stuart,
daughter of Lord
Stuart de Rothesay

Henry Lascelles,
*4th Earl of
Harewood*
(1824–92)

m. 1845, Lady
Elizabeth de Burgh,
daughter of the
1st Marquess of
Clanricarde

Hubert de Burgh,
*2nd Marquess of
Clanricarde*
(1832–1916)

King George V
(1865–1936),
m. 1893, when Duke
of York

HRH Princess
Victoria Mary of
Teck (1867–1953),
Queen Mary

Henry Lascelles
*5th Earl of
Harewood*
(1846–1929)

m. 1881, Lady
Florence Bridgeman,
daughter of the
3rd Earl of Bradford

Henry Lascelles,
*6th Earl of
Harewood* KG
(1882–1947)

m. 1922, HRH the
Princess Royal,
daughter of
King George V

George Lascelles,
*7th Earl of
Harewood*
(born 1923)

m. 1967
Patricia Tuckwell

Harewood House, north front, by Thomas Malton, c. 1788

Left Edwin Lascelles, by Sir Joshua Reynolds, 1795
Right Edward, 1st Earl of Harewood, by Sir Joshua Reynolds, 1762

Harewood House, north front, by J. M. W. Turner

Harewood House from the southeast, by J. M. W. Turner

Harewood House from the southwest, by J. M. W. Turner

Left Edward Viscount (Beau) Lascelles, by H. Edridge, 1805
Right John Carr, by W. Beechey

Chesterfield House, the London home of Viscount Lascelles
from 1919–32

The Library at Chesterfield House

Left Robert Adam, artist unknown

Right Louisa, Countess of Harewood, by George Richmond

Terrace and lake at Harewood, 1860

The Old Library

The Library

The Gallery

The Dining Room

no mean order. In the management of the home farm under his charge, he may set an example of profitable high farming; and in his daily intercourse with tenant farmers, he can easily throw out hints which will prove of great practical benefit to them. . . .'

An earlier manual, *On the Management of Landed Estates*, published in 1806, advised the additional qualifications of land-surveying, mechanics, 'a competent knowledge of rural architecture' and 'a thorough knowledge of accounts'. Besides these, a resident manager 'should be a man of fair character, of upright principles and conciliatory manners, to set an example of good conduct to the tenants, and to become their common counsellor and peace maker in those trifling disputes which never fail to arise among the occupiers of adjoining lands, and which too frequently bring on serious quarrels and law suits. . . .' The author, W. Marshall, did not forget to list, as guidance for the landowner, the attributes of the desirable tenant – capital, skill, industry and character, in that order. 'For farms of size, as those of one to five hundred pounds a year, the occupier ought to have, at his command, from five hundred to a thousand pounds of capital for every hundred pounds of rent. On the majority of farms, the former proportion is too small to manage them with full profit.'

Rents were payable half yearly, at Ladyday and Michaelmas, and a typical lease reserved the right of the landowner to work mines and quarries on the land, to fell timber, to plant, remove or alter hedges and to alter the line of roads, among other powers. Road maintenance, both of private and public highways – except, usually, toll roads – was also an important part of the landed proprietor's duties. In northern and some midland counties these were normally made of broken quarry stones laid upon a firm and even base of sand, fine gravel and occasionally faggots of brushwood or long branches of heather; in southern counties the surface was usually of flints or other hard stones. Flints cemented with chalk, noted Marshall, 'form the most useful and durable roads of this island'. Manuals like Marshall's laid down recommended sizes of roadstone – 'none shall exceed four inches, three and a half inches being the median' – which were sifted with a 'gage' or iron ring attached to a short handle, something like a glassless magnifying glass.

Marshall's pioneering work remained for many years the bible of an occupation which did not gain full professional recognition until 1902, when the Land Agents' Society was founded. Professional qualifications through examinations were not introduced until the 1920s. Meanwhile, as the historian F.M.L. Thompson has noted in *English Landed Society in the Nineteenth Century*, the work of the land agent became progressively more exacting with the increase of land enclosures, the long-drawn-out negotiations over purchase of land by the railway companies (Lord Harewood was involved in negotiations with more than a dozen in Yorkshire, at enormous legal cost), and the growth of tenants' rights. Nor, although he was highly paid at the end of the eighteenth century, did his salary improve much, if at all, during the succeeding century with all its complex new challenges; £1000 a year was not all that common as late as 1929.

The agent could, however, enjoy considerable vicarious esteem in county society; hunting several times a week with the master's pack or serving as a county magistrate. He acted as a kind of alter ego, attending tenants' weddings on behalf of the landlord or organizing election campaigns for him. A few ran substantial businesses of their own, managing several estates or even owning a coal mine, like Hugh Taylor, chief agent to the Duke of Northumberland from 1847 to 1865, who figured in a kind of regional *Who's Who* of 1895 called *Men of Mark 'Twixt Tyne and Tweed*. Agents, unlike stewards – occasionally the titles were interchangeable – were classed as gentlemen and often lived in considerable style, as indeed did Lord Harewood's agents earlier this century, with their own household staff including a butler and coachman. (When Harewood village was rebuilt as part of Carr's design for an architecturally integrated estate, the agent's and doctor's houses were immediately recognizable by their height and pedimented façades.) Some were intellectually distinguished and would have made a mark in any occupation. One celebrated agent in the nineteenth century was Rowland Prothero, a lawyer and writer with a Balliol degree and fellowship of All Souls who served the tenth Duke of Bedford as agent-in-chief. He rose to become an MP in the Asquith parliament of 1914 and President of the Board of Agriculture and Fisheries in 1916. He was largely responsible for securing guaranteed prices for farm produce during the First World War and established a minimum wage for the farm labourer. Eventually he reached the ranks of the peerage himself, being created Baron Ernle by Lloyd George in 1919. His *Who's Who* entry in 1936, the year before he died, listed a town house in Cheyne Walk, Chelsea, a manor in Berkshire, membership of the Athenaeum Club, a score of honorary doctorates and scholarly publications, but ignored all mention of his time managing the Duke of Bedford's estates. Yet Prothero's position was hardly a servile one; estates as large as the Bedford domain had a sizeable bureaucracy to manage their affairs, with sub-agents reporting to the agent, bailiffs to collect the rents and specialist managers for forestry, game, farm management and other departments. In such cases the agent was enabled, if he so wished, to lead almost as elegantly leisured a life as his proprietor.

That life, in Yorkshire as in many other counties, had not until the end of the eighteenth century been distinguished by much culture or education. There were exceptions of course, but in mid-Georgian England, drinking, gambling and blood sports were the main recreations of the country squire, just as bull and bear baiting, cock fighting, goose riding and badger baiting were the grisly sports of the villager. Harewood had its iron bear-baiting ring, stocks and pillory near the junction of the Wetherby and Leeds–Harrogate roads. The development of horse racing and cricket, commented one Yorkshire historian earlier this century, was good for a man's soul; they were sports of which no Christian need be ashamed, though 'many Christian men ought to have been bitterly ashamed of setting cocks to fight, and dogs to draw badgers'. In the mid-1750s, wrote J.S. Fletcher in 1918,

> one is obliged to set down the average Yorkshire gentleman's amusements and recreations as having been of a gross and Pagan nature. . . . Not even the upper classes were educated. The country gentleman could do little more than scrawl his own name . . . if his wife could cast up the household expenses book it was as much as was expected of her.

The Lascelles, Fitzwilliams and other Yorkshire aristocrats hardly fell into this category, but for all their libraries, paintings, subscriptions to the opera and commissioning of works of art they were also countrymen with a passion for racing and hunting. York racecourse had been opened as early as 1731, and the Lascelles were dedicated hunting men – two earls were to die on the hunting field – as were their neighbours the Lane-Foxes of Bramham Park, with whom they shared decades of mastership of the Bramham Moor Hunt. James (Jemmy) Lane-Fox, founder of the hunt in the 1770s, was a pioneer of hound breeding and remained master of the hunt until failing health forced him to give up in 1822. Henry, second Earl of Harewood, succeeded the colourful Squire Jemmy as MFH, since Jemmy's son George had no interest in hunting; the hounds were kennelled at Harewood House for more than twenty years and then reverted to Bramham Park in 1848 along with the mastership. The Bramham Moor Hunt, which still flourishes today, was always reckoned a stiff test of horsemanship, meeting four times a week over country ranging from ploughland to pasture, moors to woodland, with ditches on the York and Ainsty side and at Selby, and walls on the Harrogate side. Hunting was an expensive business; in 1820 it was costing Lord Harewood about £1800 a year. The novelist Anthony Trollope, a reliable guide to many mores of the nineteenth-century country gentry, reckoned in his *Autobiography* that at least two thousand a year was needed to maintain a hunt which went out four days a week.

Field sports aside, the country house year was measured out with magistrate's duties in the county town (quarter sessions was a social occasion liberally garnished with balls and parties), with hunt balls, subscription balls, and private dances, with visits to other country houses and, for the wives, with helping the poor and sick of the parish and administering the village school, which might well, as at Harewood, have been paid for by the landowner. Some landlords, like Lord Harewood, still presided over their old manorial courts or 'leets' twice a year, held at Harewood in the schoolroom around Easter and Michaelmas. Fines up to forty shillings were imposed for a variety of minor offences – a far cry from the trip to Gallows Hill meted out by Harewood's medieval lords of the manor – and local constables sworn into office. In districts which enjoyed such amenities, there were also the visits to spas, which in late Georgian and Regency England were emerging as places where one not only took therapeutic treatment for the long winters of too much port and madeira, but preened among fashionable society, made matches for daughters and gratified a wife's social aspirations. Harrogate's springs of sulphur, magnesia, saline and chalybeate waters had been known since the sixteenth century; by the reign of George III the small town, still little more than a village, was being patronized by Yorkshire gentry seeking relief for diseases from gout to nervous debility, and its two leading hotels, the Granby House and the Green Dragon, were known respectively as the House of Lords and the House of Commons. (A third, the Queen's Head, was disparagingly dubbed the Manchester Warehouse on account of its popularity with businessmen from that city.) Country house life itself held great stretches of tedium, especially for the non-bookish who could not even find solace in the library; for some, the customary round of riding, shooting, paying and receiving calls, evenings at cards after a lengthy formal dinner, crawled as slowly and hypnotically as a lizard. The Duke of Wellington commented caustically on 'the immense waste of time in the manner of passing the day. . . . I who have been engaged in business, commanding armies, or something of that sort, can scarcely conceive how people contrive to pass their time so totally without occupation.'

At Harewood, however, life was certainly not lacking in interest for the landowner and his family in the early years of the nineteenth century. The village, for one thing, was being rebuilt in keeping with the classic architecture of Carr's and Adam's mansion. Exact dates are difficult to pin down; there is hardly any documentation on what must have been a major exercise in town planning. At one time it was thought that the old village of Gawthorpe clustered around the church and was moved several hundred yards as the park of Harewood House was extended, forming the T-shaped layout we see today. But in May 1962 students of Leeds University on a fieldwork course based on the Harewood archives concluded not only that the rebuilding took place later than usually supposed, somewhere between 1796 and 1812, but that the village layout had changed very little over the centuries. By comparing maps made around 1690, 1796, 1812 and 1850, they found no evidence that it had ever encircled the church, although the gale of 1962 had brought down many 150-year-old trees on the north side of Church Lane, revealing large masses of worked stone among the tree roots. This confirmed that houses had once stood there, though they do not appear on the 1812 map, so these villagers may have been moved in the rebuilding. On the whole, however, the students concluded that the pre-Carr village of 1690 was not unlike that of today in its layout; there was a scatter of houses south of the castle where the medieval bondmen had lived (the terrace is still known as Bondgate) and a symmetrical line of houses corresponding to the present Avenue. There had also been houses on the western side of the Leeds road which were evidently pulled down to make room for the park extension and the building of the Doric park entrance, designed by Carr and executed in 1801 by John Muschamp, the village mason.

The new houses, consisting for the most part of four small rooms, were built in uniform blocks of three or four with semicircular arches over the windows, a Carr trademark, and long front gardens bounded by a continuous stone wall about three feet above road level. From the position of the old houses along the Avenue, it seems likely that the new ones were built behind them, causing minimum discomfort to the tenants, who simply moved a few yards into the new model dwellings; the old ones would then have been demolished and the gardens laid out. Disruptive as the rebuilding would have been, it was probably nothing to the effect on the lives of villagers of the early nineteenth century enclosures, which reached a peak in 1811. The Enclosure Acts, which replaced the old common land rights of the peasant farmer with regulated, bounded fields drawn up at the landowner's behest, made farming more economic and productive and enormously increased the value of the rent-roll, but they impoverished many yeomen with inadequate compensation and were a source of bitter resentment in agricultural communities.

Harewood gradually settled into its new clothes, and with the dignified new frontages came a quieter, more decorous mode of village life. The bear-baiting ring disappeared with the market cross and the stocks when the Wetherby road was levelled in 1804. The village pond was filled in – the depression in the ground can still be seen beyond the last house on the north side of the Avenue. The six old pubs, most of them little more than rooms set aside for drinking in private houses, disappeared to make way in 1810 for the trim Georgian architecture of the Harewood Arms; 'fitted up in a neat and commodious manner', as the guidebook remarked, 'the rooms are well furnished with new beds and bedding, the cellars are well stored with liquors; good post-chaise, able horses, and careful drivers are at command.'

Village life, however, remained at bottom the same; its occupations, despite Edwin Lascelles's well-intentioned experiment with ribbon manufacture, tied to the land and its animals, the estate and the domestic needs of the community. In 1818 John Jewell, the author of the guidebook, put the population at 854, principally 'farmers, shopkeepers, artisans and labourers; the latter of whom are constantly employed by the Earl of Harewood'. (About a quarter of the population worked for the estate.) The village was actively Methodist as early as 1772, with services held in private houses – two of which were converted in 1815 into a chapel. There was also a strong Quaker influence.

Harewood quickly gained a reputation as a model of the new town planning. 'Harewood may be distinguished from almost every other village in the kingdom,' wrote Jewell, who admittedly was not an unbiased observer, 'by its regularity and cleanliness . . . uniformly and modestly rebuilt, so as to exclude every appearance of filth or poverty. The whole of the town is built with fine stone, procured from the neighbouring quarries, and even the cottages possess a look of neatness bordering upon elegance, while the principal houses assume an air of superiority that accords with the vast domain to which they appertain, and reflect the liberal mind which erected them.' Among benefits indisputably gained by the rebuilding was the supply of good water to the houses from a reservoir near Stockton constructed by the earl at his own expense. In 1814, Jewell recorded, Lord Harewood had also 'apportioned a considerable quantity of good pasture and arable land to the cottagers, for gardens, and those who best cultivate their portions receive great encouragement.'

The ruling family had, some fifty years before, built a village school with two houses for the teachers; a bigger one, again entirely financed by the Lascelles, was put up in 1845. The trend to self-improvement, by then spreading out from the Leeds in which Samuel Smiles was lecturing to artisans, also prompted the Lascelles to provide a Literary and Scientific Institution, with reading room, library of eight hundred volumes, lectures and evening classes. In 1819 the first earl funded twenty scholars to study free; his second son Henry, who became the heir, paid for twelve; Henry's wife subsidized fourteen girls and the earl's daughter two girls.

The old coarse village sports were slowly superseded by cricket matches, visits from touring drama companies, dances and holiday feasts. Communications were improving. Jewell reported proudly that 'the Telegraph coach goes through Harewood every morning about six o'clock on its way from Leeds to Sunderland, and returns the same evening about seven o'clock . . . this village is well provided with carriers to all parts of the country. . . . The Post comes into this village every morning about three o'clock (Tuesday excepted from London) and goes out to all parts the same evening at six o'clock.'

Up at the big house, meanwhile, work progressed in leisurely fashion on finishing the park landscaping set in train by Capability Brown. Again, dates are elusive, but by 1851, when the first Ordnance Survey map was made of the area, the medieval fields which had bordered the Leeds–Harrogate road had been swallowed up within the park, and new plantations and driveways laid out. Humphry Repton, the distinguished landscape designer who worked all over England in the early nineteenth century and provided beautiful 'before and after' sketches for his clients in the 'Repton Red Books', made some suggestions – few of them carried out – for the park and for extending the house. Repton's design for the park gates was rejected, to his chagrin, and Carr's chosen instead. Jewell in his guide to the estate mentions a park of 1800 acres, but there is no evidence to suppose it was more than 800 acres by the time its boundaries were finally drawn. As the park expanded northward, the old line of the Leeds–Harrogate turnpike – which originally turned left just after the present entrance gates, passed the vicarage (the present Estate Office) and then turned right down the hill to the bridge – was pushed out and round the base of the hill along the route it follows today down Harewood Bank.

By the turn of the nineteenth century, Harewood was already a fixture on the knowledgeable traveller's map of England. Joseph Farington made a special diversion from Leeds on a five-week journey north to Scotland in August 1801:

> Saw Lord Harwood's [*sic*] House. It is built of stone and is beautifully situated on the side of sloping ground, at the bottom of which a fine river passes. The view of the country is very extensive, and exhibits all the riches of cultivation. The House is a very good one, and the rooms comfortable and seem made for use.

The art collections, however, had scarcely begun: Farington noted that the only pictures were the four paintings by Zucchi, some landscapes and local views and family portraits by Reynolds, Singleton and Hoppner. Jewell's 1819 guide reveals how the taste of the first earl had stamped itself on the interior; not yet a treasure house of art, it nevertheless displayed the personality of an educated squire with a lively interest in things of the mind. The library had expanded from Edwin Lascelles's day to about four thousand books in a variety of languages. The room also contained a billiard table, two glass cases with models of French warships and, in wall niches above, busts of Newton, Machiavelli, Dante, Petrarch, Boccaccio and Sappho. The passage outside was lined with maps and paintings of favourite dogs. The earl's dressing room had more literary busts – Shakespeare, Milton, Pope and Johnson – as well as views of foreign seaports and hunting scenes and portraits of the Duke of Wellington, William Pitt the Younger, who had recently died, and the late Countess of Harewood, a Yorkshirewoman from Guisborough, who had left the earl a widower in 1805.

Jewell, the Harewood porter, was inspired to write his guide because Harewood House was already open to the public every Saturday from 11 a.m. to 4 p.m. and during the spa season was a popular day excursion from Harrogate. Jewell's book remains surprisingly vivid and readable today, taking the twentieth-century reader in his footsteps around the house and grounds when they were still comparatively new. We marvel with him at such vanished glories as the Circular Room (demolished by Sir Charles Barry in the 1840s), twenty feet in diameter, its domed ceiling supported on sixteen pilasters with Ionic capitals; the original 'best' staircase with its landing made of 'one solid stone, eighteen feet by six feet', and the house's seventy-six 'handsome and massy mahogany doors' – those, at least, still surviving for admiration today. Visitors were encouraged to walk around the pleasure grounds and gardens before returning to their carriages parked in front of the north entrance. The fruit gardens were particularly famous; there were hothouses for figs, peaches, pineapples, grapes and Jamaican grenadillas, and in 1818 a melon was cut that weighed twelve pounds.

The first earl commissioned some fine but strictly practical pieces of furniture from Thomas Chippendale the Younger; the pier tables he made in 1797 for the Gallery so faithfully followed his father's style that for decades they were assumed to have been part of the original furnishings of the house. The two massive mahogany 'cloathes presses' for Lord Harewood's dressing-room, also ordered from Chippendale and Haig, reflected the growing care for personal appearance and hygiene in the age of Beau Brummell, as did the heavy cheval mirror balanced in its mahogany stand, and the accoutrements ordered for his lordship's bathroom. But the hand that directed Harewood's art collections was that of Beau Lascelles, who developed a considerable reputation as a connoisseur before his death in 1814 at the age of fifty. His flair was chiefly for porcelain – he began the great Sèvres collection at Harewood, maintaining an account with a Bond Street dealer called Robert Fogg and spending hundreds of pounds in a year – but also in his patronage of artists. An amateur painter of talent himself, as Farington had noted, Lascelles was strongly influenced by the work of Thomas Girtin, whom he invited to Harewood along with two other young painters working in watercolour, J.M.W. Turner and John Varley. It was an inspired idea; the three produced a topographical record of a great house and its landscape that combined surpassing beauty with unique documentary value.

Viscount Lascelles's death in early middle age while still a bachelor meant that Henry, the second son and the family's most active political figure, became the heir. Seven years earlier, in 1807, Henry Lascelles had taken part in a famous electoral battle between two great Yorkshire families for a county seat, the first to be contested in Yorkshire since 1742. Catholic emancipation was the burning issue of the election and Lascelles, the Tory, campaigned against it, while his Whig opponent, Lord Milton, the heir to Earl Fitzwilliam, supported reform. But both were up against the great Evangelical reformer William Wilberforce, who had been returned for Yorkshire time after time. Wilberforce's crowning achievement, the bill abolishing slavery, had just passed into law and he was at the zenith of his reputation; the 'authorised interpreter of the national conscience', as the *Dictionary of National Biography* expressed it. Nevertheless, he won the 1807 election by only 629 votes over Milton, with Lascelles a close third. The polling lasted fifteen days and each of the aristocratic candidates spent more than £100,000, compared with Wilberforce's £28,600, raised by public subscription; Lascelles' campaign expenses included a bill from the George Inn at York for £1763 15s. 3½d. for entertaining his supporters and repairing the damage they did to furniture and windows. Lascelles subsequently found a safer seat at Westbury in Wiltshire. In 1812 both Milton and Lascelles were returned for Yorkshire county seats but in 1818 Lascelles retired to take over his family's 'pocket borough' seat of Northallerton; two years later he became the second Earl of Harewood. Politics was his ruling interest and he had less time for the arts than his brother or father. During his ownership the house was little changed but became a social hub of the West Riding where the earl, as Lord Lieutenant, entertained notable visitors to the county, including, in September 1835, the young Princess Victoria and her formidable mother, the Duchess of Kent.

There had been royal visits in the first earl's time; Queen Charlotte and the Prince Regent had come in 1815 to see the Harewood porcelain and Grand Duke Nicholas of Russia, later Tsar Nicholas I, came in the winter of 1816 with a retinue of eighteen, putting up at Greaves' Hotel in Leeds before inspecting the woollen factory of Wormald, Gott and Fountaine, a flax-spinning mill and an ironworks. At Harewood House the Russian party was received in splendid state, the servants in full livery lining the hall and a great assembly of local nobility and gentry waiting to be introduced. Dinner was served on the famous Lascelles gold plate and a concert almost entirely composed of Handel's music followed, performed by fifty musicians and the Harewood church choristers. The young Russian prince toured the estate next morning, expressing admiration at the industrious cottagers and remarking that it was a system that would merit his adopting at home.

Princess Victoria's visit was again an occasion for the gold and silver plate, some of the individual pieces so heavy that it was as much as one person could do to carry them to the head table. Dinner was laid for 130 and sightseers were allowed into the Gallery to glimpse the glittering tables. A troop of Yorkshire Hussars formed a guard of honour to welcome the royal party and the bells of the village church were rung continually from early in the morning. All the great local landowners – Ibbetsons, Vavasours, Fitzwilliams, Foxes – were represented, along with the new industrial rich of Leeds like Benjamin Gott, the textile manufacturer, who had had his own Palladian mansion designed for him by Robert Smirke at Armley Park, within sight of his smoking mill chimneys. On this occasion the guest of honour was too fatigued after her journey from York and elaborate luncheon in the music room to join an afternoon tour of the estate by carriage. Next morning, however, the patience of hundreds of sightseers was rewarded by the sight of the royal party walking to Sunday service at the parish church, where the Archbishop of York preached a minatory sermon from St John's Gospel on the text 'The night cometh when no man can work'.

In 1835 Lord Harewood received the last £10,000 of his £100,000 inheritance, paid by means of a block of consols, and the following year his finances were further improved by compensation of £26,000 for the freeing of 1276 slaves on his West Indian plantations. The family continued to maintain its handsome style of life, divided between Yorkshire and London, where the second earl spent much time at the House of Lords. Travel was still a cumbersome business: the 200-mile journey north involved changes of horses at Barnet, Welwyn, Baldock, Eaton, Stilton, Stamford, Colsterworth, Grantham, Newark, Tuxford, Barnby Moor, Doncaster and Ferrybridge, and as many as six nights at stopovers at such hostelries as the Castle and Falcon at Newark, which boasted on its engraved bill-head: 'Excellent well aird [sic] Beds, Stabling, Lock up Coach Houses etc.' The railway revolution was at hand, however, and these laborious logistics would soon appear distantly archaic.

5

Victorian Prosperity and Gorgeous Palaces

Queen Victoria was only twenty-two and barely four years on the throne – six years after her youthful visit to Harewood – when Henry Lascelles, the second younger son in succession to inherit, became the third earl in 1841. But already there was a palpable sense that a new age had arrived. Even if few people were yet aware of the mechanical processes that were beginning to revolutionize industry and agriculture, none could ignore the rapid and visible spread of the railway network and the way in which – only a dozen years after George Stephenson had taken the Rocket on its trials at Rainhill, near Liverpool – the train was shrinking England. Leeds to London, a journey which took the best part of a week by coach and horses, could be covered in ten hours by train in 1840; twenty years later, it would be down to four hours, little more than the motorway drive today.

Initially, it was an expensive way to travel – £2 15s. for a one-way second-class fare, which added up to a considerable sum if you were transporting twenty-five servants to London for the season, as the Lascelles family did, plus the cost of omnibus or hackney cab at either end. But the journey by road, with nine horses and two carriages, cost £80. As railway travel developed in efficiency, the financial savings became enormous for country-dwelling aristocrats who moved their entire households to London and back once a year.

A pamphlet published in Doncaster in 1863 gave some graphic examples: a nobleman living in south-west Scotland would have to spend £350 to move his family of twelve and ten servants the 405 miles to London by horses and carriages. The journey took six days in winter, five in summer. By rail it could be accomplished in fifteen hours and cost £107 10s. each way – a saving of £485 in a year. A married couple travelling the 162 miles from Doncaster to London, accompanied by a servant each and paying a premium to have their private carriage drawn by fast post horses, would have to pay £21 19s. – by rail, the cost was £7 16s. The mail-coach fare was £1 10s. for an outside seat, £3 for an inside one, but the additional obligatory disbursements for the guard, the coachman and expenses on the road, could add another £2. The trip from Doncaster took twenty-one hours by mail coach; stagecoach was cheaper but took three hours longer. The train covered the distance in four hours and cost a mere £1 7s. 6d. first class.

Yorkshire, of whose broad expanse it was said there were as many acres as there were letters in the Bible, was the cradle of the railway industry: Doncaster and York grew into great manufacturing centres for the rolling stock of the Great Northern and North Eastern companies respectively, and the infinity of green acres was crossed by one iron track after another throughout the 1830s and 1840s. Landowners grew rich on the railway boom; not only was land wanted by the competing companies but the letting value of farmland could rise by anything from 5 to 20 per cent according to the proximity of a railway station. In the 1860s the increase was reckoned at about 7 per cent if the station was within five miles. Landowners also invested heavily in the new industry: the personal bank books of the earls of Harewood during Victoria's reign record regular dividends from a clutch of railway companies at home and abroad, including the Brighton Railway, the North Eastern, the North Western and the Grand Trunk Railroad of Canada, as well as investments in St Katharine's Docks in London and the inevitable consols.

Initially, many landowners were hostile to the encroachment on their estates and resentful of the effect of the steaming, clanking locomotives on their livestock and game. Some used their influence in Parliament to get lines diverted from their land; others accepted bribes for *not* using such influence. Land still spelled power and it was not until 1885 that the landed gentry were outnumbered in the House of Commons by manufacturers and businessmen. Earl Fitzwilliam, head of a famous old Yorkshire family, managed to get the Great Northern diverted by a quarter of a mile in order to preserve his fox-hunting near Peterborough. The third Earl of Harewood had his say over the siting of a railway, much as his predecessor had done on the proposed routing of a public highway through his park. Local folklore has it that the viaduct and tunnel carrying the Leeds–Harrogate line at Arthington were moved from their planned position because they encroached on Harewood land: the railway was certainly the subject of correspondence and meetings between Lord Harewood's agent and the engineer of the Leeds and Thirsk Railway Company in the winter of 1845/46, but the tunnel was eventually built under the Harewood–Otley road more or less as planned. The viaduct, seen today from the handsome, early nineteenth-century house of the Sheepshanks family at Arthington, looking west over the river valley, forms one of the finest views in Wharfedale. So widespread were the Harewood land holdings that in the dawn of the railway age the earl and his tenants were involved in negotiations at different times with no fewer than thirteen railway companies.

As the industrial towns expanded – Middlesbrough, sitting on a thick bed of iron ore, became the fastest-growing town in the country, while entrepreneurs flocked to Leeds to manufacture the new machinery – so did the fortunes of the industrialists. New money was circulating in vast quantities and, in the immutable English way, its owners wanted to put it into land and country houses. Having built themselves, as the Mayor of Bradford said at the opening of the Saltaire Mill in 1853, 'palaces of industry almost equal to the palaces of the Caesars', they wanted domestic palaces in beautiful surroundings. A typical early example was Benjamin Gott, the cloth merchant of Leeds born in 1762 who became a pioneer of mechanization and worked his way up from apprentice to manage the old-established company of Wormald and Fountaine. He built the first factory in Leeds in which the entire textile process was carried out from wool to finished cloth under one roof. The firm's broadcloths, exported across the world, had a reputation for superfine quality.

Gott bought his country estate at Armley in 1803; it occupied a commanding position with sweeping views embracing both the picturesque Kirkstall Abbey, a favourite subject of Turner and Girtin, and the flaring mill furnaces of Leeds. He brought in the London architect Robert Smirke to remodel the existing house in Greek Revival style, with an imposing portico resembling a small-scale Parthenon, and commissioned Humphry Repton to design the grounds. Repton, who produced one of his Red Books for Armley (now in the possession of the Mellon family), commented shrewdly that the distance between mansion and town was likely to shrink as the latter's prosperity increased; today, Leeds entirely encircles the peeling remains of Gott's Acropolis on its hill. Repton also had a hand in the interior of the Gott mansion, believing that 'the great world of London must be copied at the distance of two hundred miles'. His catalogue of indispensable furnishings reads like the worst excesses of Victoriana, though the Victorian age still lay some years in the future: 'organs, pianofortes, and harps, and tables of every kind . . . cabinets and sophas [*sic*], and footstalls [*sic*], and music stands, and workboxes, and flower pots, and clocks, and bronzes, and cut glass, and China, and Library-tables; covered with books, and pamphlets, and reviews, and newspapers; which contribute to the elegant and rational enjoyment of modern life.' Gott enjoyed his position in society, mingled with local aristocrats like the Lascelles and devoted his old age to philanthropic works and patronage of the arts.

Leeds, now rapidly transforming itself from the modest cloth-market town described by Daniel Defoe in his *Tour Through the Whole Island of Great Britain* to a powerhouse of the industrial revolution, personified the age of the inventive, energetic entrepreneur and that layer of society which became known as the 'millocracy'. Within thirty years, from 1801 to 1831, the town's population more than doubled from 52,302 to 123,546 (by 1861 it would be over 200,000), and as early as 1811 Louis Simond, a Frenchman arriving in Leeds from America, noted that 'from a height, north of the town . . . a multitude of fires issuing, no doubt, from furnaces, and constellations of illuminated windows spread upon the dark plain.' In the 1820s a German princeling observed the 'transparent cloud of smoke' covering the whole area of Leeds, and that 'a hundred red fires shot upward into the sky, and as many towering chimneys poured forth columns of black smoke. The huge manufactories, five storeys high, in which every window was illuminated, had a grand and striking effect. Here the toiling artisan labours far into the night.' By 1831, a lady visitor noted, both Leeds and Bradford were smoky places of 'great long chimneys . . . doubled, I think, in number within these two or three years.' By 1845, a Royal Commission was reporting dire slum conditions, many families dwelling in a single cellar room 'one mass of damp and filth . . . the floor in many places absolutely wet; a pig in the corner also.' *The Builder* magazine called Leeds a 'filthy and ill-contrived town'.

But there was an irrepressible spring of upward mobility and self-improvement. It was appropriately enough in Leeds in the 1840s that the Scottish physician and railway executive Samuel Smiles delivered the series of lectures which became the basis of his epochal *Self Help*, published in 1859. His lecture audience was a group of Leeds artisans who had formed a society for mutual improvement: Smiles found them, as he said, 'groping after some grand principle which they thought would lead them to fresh life, liberty and happiness.' He gave them the precepts of hard work, thrift and competition – 'the great social law of God' – and the book which followed was the first and most successful of all self-improvement manuals. By 1905 it had sold half a million copies and had been translated into Japanese and Arabic as well as most European languages; in 1981 it was still in print in John Murray's hardback list. The book's success was fed by the many contemporary examples of self-made fortunes, though at the time Smiles was giving his talks, conditions in Leeds favoured only the fittest: the average life expectancy was forty-four for the gentry and well-off manufacturers, twenty-seven for tradesmen and shopkeepers, and nineteen for labourers and mill operatives.

Ironically, the magnate chiefly associated with the age of railway prosperity in the north of England, George Hudson, the so-called 'Railway King', went bankrupt before he could enjoy the fruits of success as a landowner. He bought Londesborough Park, one of the finest properties in the East Riding, from the Duke of Devonshire for nearly half a million pounds, mainly to prevent the land falling into the hands of a rival railway company; then made a killing by selling back part of it to one of his own companies. He also bought a magnificent seventeenth-century house near Ripon, Newby Hall, noted for one of Robert Adam's finest interiors; became an MP and Lord Mayor of York and numbered Prince Albert among his acquaintances. But his labyrinthine speculations collapsed with the fall of railway shares in the late 1840s, his blatant practices in what would now be called insider dealing were uncovered, and he was forced to resign as chairman of five railway companies. Hudson went to live abroad while a twenty-year Chancery suit dragged on with the North Eastern Railway and, though he was somewhat rehabilitated towards the end of his life, he never succeeded in becoming a great Yorkshire landowner.

While the millocracy built or acquired great houses, the aristocracy developed a craze for remodelling and embellishing their own ancestral seats, often to the point of rendering them unrecognizable. The nobility was making money out of industrialization in many areas other than railways, through owning coal mines and quarries on their land and property in the fast-growing cities. Plain classicism for the country house was not only out of fashion, it did nothing to reflect a family's improved financial status. Accordingly the elegant simplicity of Georgian and Queen Anne architecture, which had blended discreetly into park and landscape, now disappeared beneath Italian villas, palatial frontages resembling Pall Mall clubs, or Gothic extravaganzas. Some, like the Buxton family's Shadwell Park in Norfolk, underwent this sort of transformation twice within a generation. 'You will I think be astonished when you see poor dear Shadwell again', wrote the Dowager Duchess in a letter in 1858. Lady Charlotte Guest, the wife of a Welsh ironmaster who had received a knighthood but not yet full acceptance by society, spent a large part of her husband's fortune on remodelling Canford Manor in Dorset as a way of establishing their social eminence. Meanwhile, at the peak of that society, aristocrats like the Duke of Westminster and the Marquess of Bute, enriched respectively by large stretches of London freeholds and by private coal mines, were themselves rebuilding and redesigning their houses and castles in the most ambitious styles.

Part of the sudden desire for cloud-capped towers and gorgeous palaces was undoubtedly to meet the new Victorian concepts of comfort and wellbeing in the home. Gaslight was coming in, and later, electricity; hot and cold running water and proper bathrooms; hydraulic lifts and central heating. There was an evident need for modernization. Georgian houses, too, had been designed for a different way of life; more formal, less private. They usually featured a series of impressive reception rooms for soirees and the appreciation of works of art; few rooms had specific purposes for the daily round. The Victorian country house, on the other hand, was deliberately compartmented, with smaller, cosier divisions for living designated as breakfast room, morning room, study, sitting room, gun room and so on. Below stairs, the elaborate planning was even more detailed; there were rooms for brushing the gentlemen's muddy boots, rooms for polishing the silver and trimming the oil lamps, and at least one country house – Kinmel Park in Denbighshire, built for an Anglesey copper magnate – actually had a room set aside for ironing the newspapers. 'The Victorian country house at its best', as Mark Girouard remarked, 'was a remarkable achievement of analysis and synthesis, a vast machine running smoothly and with clockwork precision, a hieratic structure as complex and delicately graduated as the British Constitution.' But in *The Victorian Country House* he also noted that this tendency to divide a house up into highly specialized compartments made the Victorian plan much less adaptable than the more open Georgian style when – as inevitably would happen – techniques of living changed yet again.

Nevertheless, one can appreciate why many Victorian landowners felt the need to remodel their forebears' design for living. As early as 1833 Sir Robert Peel was writing home with some asperity of the discomforts he was experiencing on a visit to Apethorpe, the Northamptonshire seat of Lord Westmorland.

Lord Westmorland told me that I had an excellent apartment full of comforts for my bedroom. To go to it to bed last night from the drawing-room I had to pass first through an old room of tapestry which was fitted up as a bedroom for King James I, and remains just as it was. . . . The second was a sort of morning room, with nothing particular in it. The window shutters and other parts of the room repaired with wood which had never been painted since it was put up, common deal. The third room was a long gallery, 115 feet long, that is just about twice the length of ours. Low, but rather a handsome room, without a single fire in it, and with windows certainly not excluding the air of heaven. Having passed through the whole of this, I came to another room, on opening the door of which my candle was blown out, and I felt my way back as well as I could through the gallery, in which there was no light whatever, to procure one. Having returned with my light, I came to the fourth room, a large deserted library, with all the books in confusion. . . . No fire in this. Then came a long passage. Then came my bedroom, a room with family portraits, very dark by day, looking into the quadrangle. There are four doors open into the room, two of them into passages and staircases that lead I know not where. Another into a sort of closet that has been cut out of the thickness of the wall, and seems occupied at present by nothing but spiders and rats.'

Apethorpe was bought in 1904 by Henry Brassey of the family of successful contractors who acquired estates in four counties, and was no doubt suitably modernized to ideas of Edwardian comfort.

In comparison with vast mansions like Apethorpe, Harewood's Georgian and Regency elegance was compactly designed and the house had always had an eminently liveable atmosphere. But it remained virtually as Edwin Lascelles had built it ninety years earlier, and the burgeoning young family which moved into it in 1841 needed both more space and more convenience – another floor of bedrooms to start with. The new countess, the former Lady Louisa Thynne, came from a great aristocratic family; she was the daughter of the second Marquess of Bath and had seen the family's magnificent Elizabethan seat, Long-leat House in Wiltshire, remodelled to more manageable proportions by Sir Jeffry Wyatville under her father's personal direction. Lady Louisa seems to have been as determined as her father to get the sort of house she wanted, despite the daunting problems involved. Her portrait looks as if she had the kind of forceful character to see such an enterprise through; the mouth is firm and decisive under the long, steep nose that is as typical of the Thynnes as of the Wellesleys.

The architect chosen was at the height of his professional reputation and greatly in the public eye as the man who had won the plum commission to design the new Houses of Parliament following the disastrous fire of 1834. Charles Barry's elaborately fretworked Gothic structure was already beginning to change the London skyline, and he would be knighted on its completion in 1852. Barry's forte was a massive Italianate style evolved from his youthful studies in Rome, Sicily and Florence; he had won considerable acclaim for his two Pall Mall club buildings, the Traveller's and the Reform. His domestic architecture, especially in the remodellings for which he was becoming noted, also had something inescapably public and monumental about it, so that many of his country houses look as though they have sprouted bits of the Reform Club or even, like Trentham Hall in Staffordshire, could double as Whitehall ministries.

It was Barry who enlarged and elaborated Canford for the iron-trade Guests and who rebuilt Cliveden by the Thames at Taplow for the Duke of Sutherland on a grandly formal scale. But his most spectacular remodelling had been completed in 1841, just before he took on the Harewood commission. This was Highclere Castle in Hampshire, home of the third Earl of Carnarvon, whose tastes ran to something richer than the cool classicism of his Georgian seat, itself reworked in the 1770s from an earlier design. Barry created around the old brick-built house an entirely different, heavily Italianate palace with five crenellated towers, one at each corner and one in the centre. It is hardly recognizable from the original, yet the Rev. Alfred Barry remarked in his 1867 biography of his father that, apart from extending the outer shell, all the main walls of the house were preserved: nowhere was 'the level of any floor or the opening of a window changed.' Under Barry's hand, wrote his son admiringly, 'the comparative flatness and insipidity of bare classicism' became wrought into 'a palace, rich and original in design . . . one of the most striking country seats in England.'

At Harewood, the noble simplicity of the Carr and Adam house, as
we see it now in the paintings of Turner and Girtin, must have struck
Barry in the same way – flat and insipid. It was a house 'of some scale
and pretension', conceded Alfred Barry, which possessed 'some mas-
siveness of design and merits of proportion'. What it needed was 'finish,
life and variety'. These Barry sought to provide by redesigning the
exterior like an Italian Renaissance palazzo. His first drawings, however, struck his clients as too ostentatious and were modified to give the
effect the house presents today. Barry's solution, adding an extra floor,
was to raise the wings of the house, 'altering their design so as to bring
them into greater importance and greater harmony with the centre, and
to improve the design of the centre itself, by adding a handsome balustrade, and by raising the chimney stacks to the dignity of architectural
features, so as to vary the flat and monotonous lines of the former roof.'
Little else, Alfred Barry records, was done except to embellish the pediment and elsewhere with carving to 'provide greater richness and life
which the original design wanted'. The finished effect, he concluded
with filial pride, 'was considerable'.

As well it might be, for the most important change Barry made was to
remove entirely the Adam portico from the south front overlooking the
lake, which had been such a distinctive feature in, among other paintings, the beautiful Turner watercolour in which the distant sunlit house
on its green bank echoes the golden glow of a clump of autumn trees in
the foreground. Lady Louisa seems to have had second thoughts at this
point, and tried to persuade him to retain at least Adam's columns, but
Barry insisted that 'the aspect of the South Front would be best without
them'. He replaced them with two-storey-high Corinthian columns, but
the ornate balustrading round the roofline and window balconies combined to give horizontal emphasis to the house in place of the subtly
varied profile which Carr and Adam had achieved.

Barry's design also included sweeping alterations to the grounds
immediately below the south front. In place of greensward sloping
naturally up to the portico as if to absorb the house into the landscape,
Barry laid out an Italian terrace garden as the final flourish to his palatial frontage, balustraded and capped with urns round three sides to
echo the roofline and cascading in flights of steps down to formal flower
beds, sculptures and fountains. Unlike Highclere, the site constrained
Barry to keep to the original ground plan and extend upwards. The
north front, less structurally disturbed, was enriched with ornamenta-

tion, carving and balustrades; here the main change was in the ground level, which was built up to conceal the basement storey, Carr's flight of ten steps up to the entrance being reduced to five. The conversion work began in the summer of 1844, starting with the Italian terrace, which took about four years to complete, hampered by severe winters and hard frosts. A special woven fencing had to be designed to keep out the hares and rabbits which plagued the gardeners.

Inside the house, Barry transformed the Georgian apartments with their stately air of formal entertaining into the sort of residence every Victorian magnate desired. The former series of state apartments became the Countess's personal suite and Edwin Lascelles' basement-level Coffee Room below the Music Room was turned into a typical Victorian servants' hall with a row of bells activated by mahogany levers. Men's and women's accommodation in the servants' quarters was, of course, strictly segregated. The former State Bedroom so elaborately fitted out by Chippendale became Lady Harewood's sitting room; it is still known today as the Princess Royal's sitting room after the last Countess of Harewood to live in the house as Barry planned it. The change in function of the state apartments made sense, for they were a natural extension to the original family wing of the house. The state dressing room became a breakfast room and was fitted with bookshelves which gave it a homely atmosphere. Barry was then faced with the challenge of what to do with Adam's saloon, designed as a grand reception room. He turned it into a library with imposing mahogany, brass-fitted bookcases curving to fill the delicate Adam alcoves and lining the walls. The magnificent coved ceiling, one of Adam's boldest and most intricate concepts, was left intact, as were the plaster over-mantels with their sculptured reliefs of Bacchic festivities; a daring mix of Georgian and Victorian which left later generations of Lascelles with formidable problems when trying to find suitable redecoration schemes.

The supremely Victorian contribution of Barry's interior remodelling, however, was the transformation of the former Yellow Drawing Room, Edwin Lascelles' family sitting room, into the apotheosis of nineteenth-century male conviviality, the Billiard Room. Male sanctums were a feature of Victorian country houses, separated by function in the Victorian fashion like the gun room, the smoking room, the study, but also, and most importantly, separated from the female of the species, though women did play billiards in a few progressive establishments. An added reason why they were felt to be necessary, as Mark

Girouard notes in *The Victorian Country House*, was the 'great tribes of Victorian bachelors, younger sons of large Victorian families unable to marry outside their class for snobbish reasons, and inside it for financial ones.' Entire bachelor wings were common in the larger country houses of the period, reached by their own staircases so as to avoid embarrassing encounters with women house guests or servants.

Billiards had been played for some three hundred years but it was only in the Regency period that special rooms began to be built for it; in that respect Edwin Lascelles had been well ahead of his time. Barry's decision to move the billiard room up to the main floor reflected the importance this predominantly male preserve had acquired by mid-century. Its location between the new Library and the principal drawing room – always regarded as a predominantly female area by the Victorians – would also have made it convenient as a bolt hole for smoking; the two functions were often combined, though the most common arrangement was to have a smoking room adjoining the billiard room. Some country houses had smoking rooms in towers, and most elaborately decorated – Turkish and Moorish influences were popular. The Marquess of Bute's Cardiff Castle ostentatiously had two, one for summer use and the other for winter, both in a tower 130 feet high. The pioneer of the smoking room was probably Prince Albert, who installed one at Osborne in 1845; it was marked off as a male preserve by the single monogrammed 'A' over the door, in contrast with the entwined 'V & A' which adorned every other entrance in the Queen's Isle of Wight retreat. By 1850, Mentmore Towers, Lord Rosebery's monumental pile in Buckinghamshire, had a tiny smoking room off a conservatory, but Robert Kerr's influential book of 1864, *The Gentleman's House*, implied that even by then it was by no means a common phenomenon. 'The pitiable resources to which some gentlemen are driven, even in their own houses, in order to be able to enjoy the pestiferous luxury of a cigar, have given rise to the occasional introduction of an apartment specially dedicated to the use of Tobacco.' Thirty years later, men could, in some establishments, spend hours apart from the women if they so desired, once they had left the drawing room for the library, the billiard room, the smoking room and the bachelor quarters.

At Harewood, a Drawing Room decorated in white and green now linked the Billiard Room and the Gallery, which was used then, as it still is, for the occasional formal banquet and concert, in the company of the grand family portraits by Reynolds, Hoppner and Lawrence. Barry shrewdly made few changes to the Gallery, merely installing two nineteenth-century fireplaces instead of the original single chimneypiece by Adam, an effect he considered as relieving the long perspective of the room, though later artistic opinion would regard his hand as less than an improvement. Barry's most dramatic interior change, and the one most regretted by later generations because it virtually destroyed Adam's original design, was to the Dining Room, which he deepened and heightened, abolishing in the process an arched recess to make way for a service passage. He built a butler's pantry and a china room and installed a hydraulic lift connected to the kitchens below. The Adam influence was restricted to a 1776 fireplace supported by caryatids; the one which in fact had been designed for the Gallery. Outside the Dining Room Barry built a domed lobby connecting with the Drawing Room and put in a service staircase to the kitchens. Near by, the main staircase of the house, nowadays hidden from public view within the family's quarters, was remodelled as a single flight with branching return flights rising from a half-landing. The only room to escape Barry's attentions in this part of the house was the beautiful Music Room with its painted ceiling roundels by Angelica Kauffmann echoing the pattern on the specially woven carpet. This room, with its decorative panels of classical ruins by Zucchi, Angelica Kauffmann's husband, and its dazzling chandelier like a cut-glass wedding cake, is now regarded as a pinnacle of Adam design.

Barry's alterations proved a good deal more expensive than the Harewoods had anticipated. There was a somewhat sharp exchange of correspondence between Lord Harewood's agent and the architect, whose final bill was nearly £37,000, and that did not include decorating and furnishing the remodelled interior, for which the fashionable London firm of George Trollope and Sons submitted bills for £7000. Trollope furnished Harewood's rooms in fatly upholstered Victorian comfort fit for a Forsyte, though Chippendale's furniture continued to thread its classic presence through the stuffed sofas and heavy draperies. The interior was also thoroughly renovated; fabrics reconditioned, walls and woodwork rubbed down and ornamental cornices treated with oil and a marbling effect, some features being picked out in white or rich colours.

The entrance hall was furnished predominantly in green, with heavy damask rep curtains and easy chairs upholstered to match, the effect enlivened by dyed scarlet sheepskin rugs and oriental carpets on the flagstoned floor, reminiscent of the medieval castle hall with its tapestries and scarlet cushions. Chippendale's elegant hall chairs were japanned to imitate rosewood, with gilded embellishment to the carving and crests; rosewood panels replaced the silk and brasswork on the Georgian writing tables either side of the door. Trollope's colour schemes elsewhere in the house had an heraldic richness – scarlet, crimson, blue and purple, sometimes put together in startling combinations. Fireside seats were upholstered in purple morocco leather, and in the Breakfast Room purple leather was set against crimson velvet curtains, an effect which must have proved a trifle overpowering with the morning toast and coffee. For the Drawing Room, known as the White Drawing Room although its draperies were of green and white satin damask, Trollcpe commissioned the artist Alfred Stevens, designer of the Wellington monument in St Paul's, to improve on Adam's rather repetitive pattern of stylized flowers and bells with 'a highly Artistic Decoration for Cove from Original Drawings, the 4 pannels [sic] filled with Life Size Figures emblematical of the Elements, and a large Group painting for Centre of Ceiling.' Stevens, still relatively unknown in 1852, took his time about executing the commission but eventually produced paintings of pagan gods reflecting the Italian influences which he, like Barry, had absorbed as a student; there were echoes of Michaelangelo and the frescoes at Pompeii which Stevens had sketched. Eighty years on, the sixth Lord Harewood would fill the room, by then renamed the Green Drawing Room, with magnificent Venetian paintings of the Renaissance, making one of the richest and most coordinated compositions in any English country house.

Much of Trollope's refurbishing was done at the firm's London warehouse, the furniture, mirrors and cornices being transported from Leeds by rail. The work took until the summer of 1853, completing a ten-year project which had left the Harewood finances badly depleted. They had been living beyond their reach in more ways than remodelling the house, entertaining lavishly and running the household accounts on a very loose rein indeed. In 1848, about the time the terrace was being finished, one of Lord Harewood's trustees instructed the agent to retrench for the next two years; only essential work was to be carried on. Curiously, the size of the bills did not reflect much change in the cost of labour from nearly a century before when Edwin Lascelles had supervised his team of masons and carpenters: masons received only 3s. 4d. a day, labourers about half a crown, bricklayers 3s., plasterers 4s.

and plumbers 5s. plus board. They worked a twelve-hour day, except in winter, when it was an hour shorter, and were lucky to get Christmas Day and Good Friday as paid holidays. Such was local interest in the rebuilding that one labourer was employed on three-quarter pay 'watching to keep people from injuring the stonework'.

It had been an eventful ten years for the family. In 1845, just as the building was in full swing, two sons aged sixteen and seventeen died within eight days of each other in March. The estate carpenters were taken off their regular work to make the cedarwood coffins with the result, as they noted in the estate work book, that a great deal of over-time was required. That same summer the heir, Henry, came of age and married Lady Elizabeth de Burgh, eldest daughter of the Marquess of Clanricarde, an Irish peer, and grand-daughter of George Canning, the Tory statesman. (The Clanricarde connection was to bring unexpected riches to the family through a chance encounter during the First World War.) Work on the house gave way in October and November to a great wave of ox-roasting, feasting and merry-making to celebrate the young viscount's happiness. There was an orchestral concert, a tenants' dinner and a fete in the park, all of which involved extra carpentry and the putting up and taking down of special booths and pavilions.

When Barry's palace was at last completed, Lord and Lady Harewood and their remaining children could enjoy all the modern conveniences of mid-nineteenth-century technology. There was piped hot water, a special 'ladies' bathroom', hot air central heating diffused through stone grilles in the floors, and a cluster of water closets both above and below stairs, finished, as social distinctions dictated, in french-polished mahogany for the ladies and gentlemen and unvar-nished oak for the servants. Harewood was advanced for its time in the matter of bathrooms; although most houses built after 1840 featured at least one, they tended to be equipped only with cold running water, the hot still having to be carried up in steaming jugs by servants. It was not until the 1880s that bathrooms with hot and cold water laid on were commonplace, even in modest dwellings renting for £50 a year, as one contemporary social historian recorded.

The third earl did not, unfortunately, survive long in his opulent new surroundings. In February, 1857, four years after settling the last of Trollope's bills, he was killed in a hunting accident, aged sixty. The countess died less than two years later, leaving four unmarried daugh-ters to find their way in the world. When Viscount Lascelles returned home as the fourth earl, he was already a widower at the age of thirty-three, his young Irish wife having died tragically at twenty-eight. She did, however, leave him with an heir and other children, and he lost little time in finding a second wife, the daughter of a landowner near Wakefield, to help raise the family who would, incidentally, now have a right to the Clanricarde fortune.

In any case Henry Lascelles was entering upon a solid inheritance in his own right at the peak of Victorian prosperity. Whatever the temporary financial setbacks his father had suffered during the rebuilding of Harewood, they had obviously been surmounted since 1848. A summary of the third earl's assets was prepared by auditors for his heir. It showed rental from the Yorkshire estates at £35,540; all rents had risen since 1850 and were to do so by an average of 20 per cent over the subsequent twenty years, the main increases occurring where 'improving' landlords took advantage of the new technology to modernize their drainage systems. Interest from turnpike mortgages was put in the balance sheet at £210 and income from quarries at £250. The estates in the West Indies had produced £7800 net the previous year and would yield about £6000 in the current year; estates in Buckinghamshire and Middlesex about £1000 after taxes and the expenses of the London house. Outgoings in Yorkshire were assessed at £19,000, including fixed annual payments of £2400; £2100 in pensions, donations and subscriptions, including £500 a year to the Bramham Moor Hunt; expenditure 'beyond profits' on woodlands, £400; income tax at sevenpence in the pound, £1000; rates and taxes, £260; fencing, £100; drainage, £660; audits, £660; incidentals, £554; agent, £900; game, £1000; gardens, £800; the domestic establishment, £3000; repairs, £4500, and fire insurance premiums on Harewood and Goldsborough, £127 11s. In all, the auditors calculated, the new earl could anticipate an income of 'say £18,000' – handsome indeed at a time when it was said that a man could enjoy all the conveniences and comforts London and the country could offer for ten thousand a year.

The fourth earl was of a temperament to enjoy both to the full, and seems never to have had a shortage of money to do so. His Glyn Mills bank books with their railway dividends and regular injections of money from the estate – in 1878, a fairly representative year, Harewood rents alone brought him in £11,000 – reflected credit balances varying between £5000 and £20,000 during those halcyon Victorian years. He paid his heir an allowance of £400 a year, £200 in July and £200 in

October, and allowed himself the same amount for spending money. A thoroughly clubbable man, he belonged to the Turf (fifteen guineas a year), the Marlborough (ten guineas), the Traveller's (ten guineas), the Princes (three guineas), the Carlton (ten guineas) and White's (eleven guineas), as well as being a member of Tattersall's and maintaining a string of racehorses in training with Weatherbys. In August 1880 he paid the Turf Club £2000 for some unspecified purpose, but this enormous sum – the equivalent of perhaps £100,000 in today's purchasing terms – seems scarcely to have dented his finances for the year. He travelled abroad (his accounts show an item of 4s. 6d. for a passport) and had his portrait painted in 1888 by Sir Edward Poynter, looking the very model of the stout, bearded, late-Victorian tycoon against a stylized rustic background.

He also spent money on careful maintenance of the Yorkshire home his father had so expensively modernized, installing gas in the early 1860s (the house manufactured its own supplies in a stone-built 'gas house' and an estate fire engine was prudently maintained) and improving the plumbing and heating systems. The London firm of Thomas Cubitt, which had built Osborne House for Queen Victoria and most of Belgravia's stucco terraces as speculative housing, was employed to design new chimney stacks to replace Barry's ornate creations.

'The peculiar genius of the English country house,' wrote Victoria Sackville-West in a nostalgic monograph published at the height of the 1941 Blitz, 'lies in its knack of fitting in.' She went on to excoriate those 'built to gratify the ostentation of some rich man in an age when display meant more than beauty; they were not allowed to grow with the oaks and elms and beeches; they were not true country houses at all, but a deliberate attempt to reproduce in the country the wealth and fame which their owner enjoyed in town. They were his country residence rather than his home.' The latter, at any rate, can never have been said of the earls of Harewood, even the one whose employment of Charles Barry might have aligned him in Sackville-West eyes with the owners of Chatsworth, Stowe, Blenheim, Welbeck, Bowood, Castle Howard and Wentworth Woodhouse, houses which, in her view, though undeniably splendid, 'cannot be said to melt into England or to share the simple graciousness of her woods and fields. . . .'

The Lascelles wholeheartedly enjoyed their country estate and its companionable house; they were regarded as good managers of the land and, despite the Canning connection and the family's venture into politics in the previous century, they remained outside the ring of county families whose houses regularly became centres of political intrigue and gossip at weekends. After its flurry of royal visits in the Regency, Harewood's social life seems to have been relatively unexciting in the time of the third and fourth earls. But the Edwardian age was on the horizon, and with it the last and richest manifestation of country-house life in England.

6

'Where Pleasure Fell Like a Ripened Peach'

The last years of the old queen's reign and the first years of the new king were not prosperous ones for landowners, although paradoxically it was the time when life in the great country houses was reaching its brilliant and luxurious zenith. A series of disastrous harvests in the 1870s had culminated in the worst of the century in 1879 and by 1901, when Queen Victoria died, the acreage under wheat in England had fallen to half of what it was in 1874. Labourers left the land in droves to work in the mills and factories; there was a collapse of arable farming and in the great agricultural depression of the 1880s and 1890s it seemed to many that land management had had its day. Rented farm land was showing a poor return on investment – even after the First World War rents were lower than they had been in the 1870s – and by the middle of the nineties the value of land had fallen by as much as a third. Landlords themselves were on the defensive, facing a spate of new legislation on tenant rights, game preservation and the settlement of estates; death duties, ominously, were introduced in 1894.

Some landowners began to sell out; the author Rider Haggard gave up his own small estate as uneconomic and wrote a study of the agrarian decline in *Rural England*, published in 1900. But there was no rush of buyers, even at the much reduced prices. 'Glorious domains and stately homes are offered in vain,' as the *Estates Gazette* put it. A magnificent Devon mansion called Flete, remodelled by Norman Shaw for the banker H.B. Mildmay, a member of the Baring family, and put up for sale during a financial crisis in 1894, never found a buyer at all. (After the Second World War it was converted by a cooperative association into apartments for retired people.) As the *Estates Gazette* observed in June 1892: 'Men who have made money in business and by judicious investment are getting $3\frac{1}{2}$ per cent to $4\frac{1}{2}$ per cent per annum on their spare capital seem now but little disposed to take on themselves the ownership of land to get only at the best a return of $2\frac{1}{2}$ per cent.'

Some industrialists and members of the new commercial aristocracy did take advantage of the bargains, buying, perhaps, for prestige rather than investment. (Later, it became the fashion to rent country houses for a season, and one commentator remarked acidly in the twenties that the 'new rich change their country house as easily as they change their motor car or yacht'.) Among those buying on the falling market were Colman, the mustard king, the Wills tobacco family, the chain book-seller W.H. Smith and the railway contractor Henry Brassey. Such men – 'the beerage', as they were nicknamed from the preponderance of brewing magnates – were now in the social ascendant: in Lord Salis-bury's government of 1886–92, one-third of the new peers came from the world of commerce and industry, including W.H. Smith (one of Salisbury's ministers) and the engineering and armaments king, Lord Armstrong. By 1896, a quarter of the peerage held company director-ships, and when Edward VII became king his preference for the com-pany of men like the banker Sir Ernest Cassel and the grocery magnate Sir Thomas Lipton over the old territorial aristocrats gave the final stamp of social acceptance to the self-made millionaire.

The old landed families, however, were by no means all in retreat. Many, like the Lascelles of Harewood, had money coming in from other sources than rented land – in Lord Harewood's case, from the family's West Indian plantations (though this was dwindling; in 1908 the income fell to as little as £500), as well as from a strong portfolio of railway shares and gilt-edged investments. But the fifth Earl of Harewood, Henry Ulick Lascelles, the eldest of fourteen children and grandson of the man who had remodelled the family seat so boldly in the 1840s, had to plan prudently when he inherited the title in 1892; the Harewood trustees monitored the estate finances with iron discipline. He sold some London property, investing the proceeds in international railway companies, and in 1894 sold the family's Hanover Square resi-dence to the Royal Agricultural Society, later acquiring the lease of a smaller house at 13 Upper Belgrave Street and another in Dorset Mews.

The fifth earl was forty-six when he inherited; he had been a school-boy of eleven at Eton when his father became the earl, and the interven-ing thirty-five years had been spent mainly in soldiering, hunting and maintaining a string of racehorses at Newmarket. He served in the family regiment, the Grenadier Guards, retiring with the rank of captain in 1872, and then went to India as ADC to the Viceroy, Lord Mayo. After commanding the Yorkshire Hussars for nearly seventeen years he became an ADC successively to Queen Victoria (in her Diamond Jubilee year), Edward VII – whom he grew to resemble to an uncanny degree – and George V. He made one small and unsuccessful bid for Parliament in 1871 (as a Tory, naturally) but proved more influential in county affairs, serving as Lord Lieutenant of the West Riding from the year he inherited until 1928, when he was eighty-two.

His wife, whom he married in 1881, came from another earldom, Lady Florence Bridgeman, daughter of the third Earl of Bradford. When he succeeded to the title he took out insurances on his property which seemed considerable at the time but look modest now with inflation and the value today of a unique Chippendale interior: Harewood House was insured for £17,000 and its contents for £30,000. By 1900, the family finances were sound enough for the fifth earl to add his own improving touch to the house by installing electric light, an expensive business which cost nearly £5000 spread over two years. Apart from that, little change took place in the house between 1890 and 1930.

Despite the strictures of the trustees, Lord Harewood found the money to accommodate the tastes of an Edwardian sporting aristocrat without depriving the estate of investment. At one time he used to hunt six days a week, with the Bramham Moor, the York and Ainsty, the Zetland and the Bedale. He bred thoroughbreds and eventually became a Steward of the Jockey Club. Although none of the Lascelles were spectacularly successful on the turf, the family colours – at first cardinal red with white braid and cap, later changed to black with yellow sleeves and cap – were more often first past the winning post in the fifth earl's time than in his son's. In financial terms his best year was 1907, when he made £5000 in prize money, but in 1913 he had the greater satisfaction of winning two major races, the Jockey Club Stakes and the Cambridgeshire, with a horse called Cantilever. Like yachting, his other sporting passion – he maintained a yacht called the *Dolores* – he regarded racing as a pure pleasure, irrespective of winnings: he did not believe anyone could make it pay unless they treated it as a full-time occupation, but he took it sufficiently seriously to buy a house at Newmarket in 1910.

Pleasure, of course, was the ruling factor in Edwardian country-house life, as well it might be at a moment in history when modern technology and still-abundant domestic servants combined to produce the perfect conditions for ease and comfort. Leonard Antequil, the sardonic outsider in Vita Sackville-West's brilliantly realized evocation of that society, *The Edwardians*, observes to himself as he watches the pampered guests strolling in perfect idleness on the lawns that it was 'a world where pleasure fell like a ripened peach for the outstretching of a hand'. All the busy interlocking structure of domestic labour, the house 'as self-contained as a little town' with its carpenter's shop, painter's shop, forge, sawmill, hothouses, existed 'to provide whatever might be needed at a moment's notice'. But despite the attractions of this sybaritic life, Antequil marvels that people of consequence have time to waste in such pointless pursuits, that men and women 'accustomed to the society of makers of history . . . are apparently content with desultory chatter and make-believe occupation throughout the long hours of an idle day.' Listening to the debutantes endlessly exchanging gossip about parties at the great London houses, he ruminates that these parties were 'like chain-smoking: each cigarette was lighted in the hope that it might be more satisfactory than the last.'

This jaundiced view from a fictional character outside the magic circle – Antequil was an explorer, taken up by hostesses as the fashion of the moment in 1905 – was shared by some in real life. Thomas Carlyle thought practice must be necessary to enjoy the 'elaborate idleness'. But Americans in particular were enchanted. 'Of all the great things that the English have invented,' wrote Henry James in 1879 after a visit to Lord Houghton's Yorkshire seat, Fryston Hall, '. . . the most perfect, the most characteristic, the one they have mastered most completely in all its details . . . is the well-appointed, well-administered, well-filled country house. The grateful stranger makes these reflections . . . as he wanders about in the beautiful library of such a dwelling, of an inclement winter afternoon, just at the hour when six o'clock tea is impending.'

If, as one historian has written, some eighteenth-century memoirs give the impression that England then was a 'federation of country houses', that must have seemed even more the case as the age of Victoria gave way to the racier era of Edward VII. For all the vacuous image conveyed in *The Edwardians*, country-house society did, after a fashion, help to influence government policy and diplomacy, set trends in art and literature and generally stamp a style on the age. The most famous of the country-house 'sets' were the Souls, so nicknamed by Lord Charles

Beresford at a house party at Lord Brownlow's seat, Belton House near Grantham, because, he is supposed to have said, 'you all sit and talk about each other's souls'. They included some of the wittiest and most cultivated men and women in society and at house parties they discussed the latest books, authors and exhibitions, wrote verse and plays and gave impromptu performances of them on the lawn.

House parties were occasionally put to more serious purpose, but even then, given the later Victorians' and Edwardians' accommodating attitude to discreet liaisons, they could throw up entertaining sideshows. Julian Amery gives an example in his mammoth four-volume *Life of Joseph Chamberlain*. Shortly before the death of Queen Victoria, a large party of fifty guests was assembled at Chatsworth, the Derbyshire seat of the Duke of Devonshire, ostensibly for a weekend of amateur theatricals but actually to provide cover for Chamberlain, the Colonial Secretary, to engage in frank talks on Anglo-German relations after dinner in the library with Baron von Eckardstein of the Kaiser's embassy in London. As it happened, the house party included two ardent lovers who, finding themselves confused in the vast impersonal corridors of Chatsworth, arranged that the woman would drop a sandwich to identify her bedroom door. Unfortunately, von Eckardstein was a voracious eater, accustomed to fortifying himself for bed with an entire cold fowl; prevented from doing so by the long discussions of state, he was making his way morosely to his bedroom when he spotted a sandwich lying in the corridor – and immediately pounced upon it, thereby ruining two people's weekend.

The weekend as such was only as old as the motor car, though the railways had already shortened the three to four weeks' stay in the country that was customary when visitors came by horse and carriage. Not everyone among the old aristocracy approved of the change. Lord Willoughby de Broke, writing nostalgically in 1921 of the lost sporting world of his grandfather, lamented the passing of 'the placid country society of the undiluted mid-Victorian type, before its character was destroyed by the multiplication of quick trains up to London, automobiles, kodaks, telephones, and weekend parties.' But for the hunting enthusiast the fast trains opened up virtually the whole of the British Isles; one dedicated man who lived in London contrived to attend most of the Saturday meets of the Galway Blazers by catching the Irish Mail from Euston on a Friday evening and a connecting train from Dublin to the West of Ireland the following morning. It was the advent of the car,

however, which made the Friday-to-Monday a social institution,
though many still arrived and left by train, and Monday morning would
see a great departure for the station, the ladies in rubber-tyred
broughams and the gentlemen in a rattling station bus.

At Harewood House, a proper visitors' book began to be kept soon
after the fifth earl succeeded; a small brown leather volume, it
opened in 1896, with a thick sprinkling of those territorial titles which
read more like entries in a gazetteer or *Bradshaw's* railway guide than
Debrett – 'Suffolk and Berkshire', 'Carnarvon', 'Crewe', 'Wenlock',
'Newport', 'Lichfield', 'Pembroke', 'Scarborough', 'Hastings', 'Arran',
'Harlech' and 'Exeter'. Many were related by marriage to the Lascelles
and each other. The Duke of Teck, Princess (later Queen) Mary's
younger brother, came in November 1902; in 1917, when the royal
family discarded its German titles – Saxe-Coburg-Gotha becoming
Windsor and Battenberg, Mountbatten – Teck was made Marquess of
Cambridge. May 1904 saw a glittering three-day house party of twenty
headed by the Prince of Wales, the future George V, and his wife, who
signed the book 'Victoria Mary'; and in 1908 King Edward himself
came to Harewood, an event which necessitated the family trustees
allowing the earl an extra £700 'towards expenses of the King's visit'.
Mr Nicholl, head of the firm which administered the trust, wrote
crisply, 'I can only hope that there will certainly be no extra expenditure
in the estate this year. . . .' Regular visitors, mainly in-laws, tended to
come twice a year, in spring and autumn, and their names might recur
for a quarter century: Lady Mabel Kenyon-Slaney, the Earl of Bradford's elder daughter and the Countess of Harewood's sister, came
every year from 1893 to 1930, three years before she died, and her
daughter Sybil, who never married, in due course became lady-in-
waiting to the Princess Royal.

The pattern of the country-house party repeated itself across the counties of England in those cushioned years before the First War. Twenty or
thirty guests would be average for the bigger houses, their names neatly
inscribed on cards which were slipped into small brass frames on the
bedroom doors, complemented by similar cards on the bell-indicator by
the pantry for the information of visiting maids and valets. The latter
took their place in the servants' hall hierarchy according to the rank of
their employers, sometimes to the extent of maids becoming known by
their lady's name; the Duchess of Bridgewater's maid thus being Miss
Bridgewater below stairs, much as Kensington Garden nannies in the

thirties referred to each other by the names of the families whose children they looked after. The housekeeper – who, like the cook, was always granted the courtesy title of 'Mrs' even if unmarried – would, in the grander houses, require to be as thoroughly grounded in *Debrett* as her employers: Vita Sackville-West, whose own upbringing at Knole, the Sackvilles' ancestral home in Kent, gave her a documentary knowledge of such minutiae, has the duchess's housekeeper in *The Edwardians* appropriating the previous year's copy of *Debrett* for her own room as soon as the current one is placed in her mistress's boudoir.

The whole well-oiled machinery of the household ran on servants whose individual cost, Sir Charles Petrie has recalled in *Scenes from Edwardian Life*, was generally estimated to be the same as the keep of a horse, about a pound a week. Their creed was to make life as comfortable as possible for their employers and their employers' guests, in as invisible a manner as possible. Printed cards listing their timetable of duties hung in their small, cold bedrooms: to quote *The Edwardians* again, 'wood must be cut and carried, hot-water bottles put into beds, inkstands filled, breakfast trays prepared, blinds raised or lowered; housemaids must vanish silently if surprised at their tasks, hall-boys must not be allowed to whistle, Vigeon (the butler) must wear London clothes in the country, no noise must be made anywhere lest her Grace should hear it and be annoyed. . . .' Each evening the lady's maid was faced with the formidable task of preparing her mistress for public display in the three-quarters of an hour customarily allowed between the sounding of the dressing-gong and appearance in full fig downstairs, successively sliding on silk stockings, heavily boned stays, suspenders, pads of pink satin for hips and underarms to accentuate the wasp waist, drawers, petticoat tied with tapes, and finally the gown itself – all this after looping and swathing the elaborate coiffure over its infrastructure of pads to which the hair would be anchored by an arsenal of hairpins. The labour quotient of an Edwardian household, despite electricity and modern plumbing, differed little from that of a century before; grates were still blacked by hand, coals still humped in heavy brass scuttles, bathrooms still scarce enough for hot water to be carried to rooms.

Dinner, which had progressively moved back in time from 2 p.m. in the eighteenth century to 8.30 or 9 p.m. in the Edwardian decade, was the climax of 'upstairs' life in the country house, and guests moved ceremoniously in pairs along a carefully mapped-out 'Dinner Route'; the women in their silks and jewels, the men in tails with black waistcoats, unless going to a dance, when white was *de rigueur* (dinner jackets were rare and still referred to disparagingly as 'bum-freezers' until the Prince of Wales popularized them after the war). At some houses noted for boisterous practical jokes, the men might be lucky to escape the literally irritating practice of having a mustard leaf sewn into the crutch of their evening trousers. (Sodium in chamber pots, which exploded on contact with water, was another popular jape, as were apple-pie beds and pillows smeared with flour.) The multi-layered Edwardian menus must have seemed daunting to tightly corseted ladies, but one was free to take a little from each dish or none at all.

The disposition of guests around the long table laden with silver and trails of smilax (luncheon was often served at small tables, restaurant style), and which gentleman should escort which lady into the dining room, was an exercise in social and diplomatic niceties, worked out by the hostess with the aid of a leather pad into which the name cards were slotted. Even more important for the reputation of a hostess was her unspoken understanding of who was whose current lover on the weekend circuit and her ability to allocate bedrooms in subtle proximity so as to avoid the desperate straits resorted to at Chatsworth. A professional bachelor of the kind who flourished in pre-1914 London society would not return to town with good reports of his weekend if placed in a bedroom amid others occupied by wives all firmly accompanied by their husbands.

The more serious pleasures of the house party, especially at houses like Harewood in good hunting and shooting country, were concerned with the pursuit of furred or feathered prey across the moors and coverts, and in the Lascelles household the autumn and winter months were busy with guests. King Edward, though an enthusiastic shot, was not in the same class as his heir. George V, who was to visit Harewood many times after his daughter married into the Lascelles family, was a legendary performer at the butts, on one occasion in Berkshire bringing down thirty-nine birds with thirty-nine successive cartridges, a particularly remarkable feat considering that he always used hammer guns, which had to be cocked by the loader. Some phenomenal bags were recorded at shooting parties before the First War; at the shoot where King George made his thirty-nine consecutive hits, on Lord Burnham's estate at Beaconsfield in December, 1913, seven guns between them accounted for 3937 birds.

Lord Harewood's heir, Harry Lascelles, grew to maturity at the high noon of Edwardian luxury and confidence. Born at Harewood House in 1882, he was the last heir to enjoy the traditional feudal celebrations at his coming of age in 1903. The West Riding tenants gave him a magnificent silver bowl weighing 425 ounces and decorated with repoussé shields representing the four seasons of farming; ploughing, sowing, reaping and harvesting. Those from the North Riding contributed a handsome dressing case of crocodile skin with solid silver fittings. Four hundred tenants were entertained to luncheon and their wives to tea. It poured with rain and the earl opened the Gallery for his guests, who were as grateful for the shelter as for the artistic treat. The last time a Viscount Lascelles had attained his majority, in 1845, it was celebrated with a medieval-style ox-roasting and the distribution to tenants of a thousand loaves and twenty butts of ale. The next time it would happen, in 1944, the heir would be a German prisoner of war in Colditz Castle.

Harry Lascelles went through the customary family sequence of Eton, Sandhurst and the Grenadier Guards before the posting as military attaché in Rome that developed his love of European art and his remarkable flair as a collector. For five years, as Edwardian England moved placidly into the new Georgian era, he served in Canada as ADC to the Governor-General, Lord Grey, before, like his father, making an unsuccessful stab at Parliament as Unionist candidate for Keighley. The issues of Unionism and Irish home rule were generating high passions; it was the era of Sir Edward Carson's threatened rebellion in the North of Ireland and the dangerously divided loyalties which culminated in the so-called Curragh Mutiny, when British army officers in Ireland under General Sir Hubert Gough declared they would resign their commissions sooner than take up arms against Ulstermen in revolt. But even as Asquith's Cabinet agonized over the Irish question in the last days of June 1914, the map of Europe was breaking up under its averted eyes. War, and the involvement of Great Britain in what had seemed to almost everyone an obscure quarrel in the Balkans, no more serious than others which had preceded it, shattered the certainties of English life in all classes. For the fighting men, among whom were early counted the cream of the young aristocracy, change was immediate and cataclysmic; the appalling experiences of Flanders and Gallipoli opened an abyss over which no bridge could ever be thrown to the old world. For those left at home change came more slowly, but great social movements were at work, like geophysical plates shifting together under the earth. They had begun, indeed, under the placid surface of Edwardian life; landowners caught an unnerving whiff of things to come with Lloyd George's 'People's Budget' of 1909 when the Chancellor, introducing a land tax which in the end was to prove unworkable, declared menacingly: 'We will give the great landlords a turn on the wheel and put them on the treadmill for a short time, and see how they like it.' War made certain that nothing would be certain again.

At Harewood, the last big, glittering house party of the old order took place in February 1914, when the recently married Prince and Princess Arthur of Connaught, cousins of the king, came with a party of twelve. In that fateful August, as Britain stumbled into war, only one visitor was recorded, the Harewoods' eldest daughter Margaret Selina, who had married the ninth Viscount Boyne in 1906. It was, though she could hardly have known it, the end of the age of idleness for daughters of the aristocracy; years later, a family servant recalled Lady Boyne being horrified that her granddaughter Rosemary wanted to take a job. When Rosemary retorted by asking what she had done with her time when young, the old lady was somewhat lost for an answer: 'We hunted, and went to balls. . . .'

Hunting and balls were over too, for a time anyway, for Viscount Lascelles, who was thirty-two when war broke out. He fought a very brave war in the Grenadiers and was wounded three times, at Givenchy, Poperinghe and the Somme. In November 1918 he commanded the third battalion of the Grenadiers when it captured Mauberge; he won the Distinguished Service Order twice (the second Lascelles son, Edward, also won the DSO with the Rifle Brigade), the Croix de Guerre, and was mentioned in dispatches. His dashing war record, coupled with a windfall inheritance of more than £2 million from his eccentric great-uncle the Marquess of Clanricarde, made him, as the twenties opened, one of the most eligible bachelors in the kingdom. In 1919 he had also become the owner of one of London's grandest residences, using some of the Clanricarde fortune to acquire Chesterfield House in South Audley Street and to reassemble many of the works of art collected by its original owner, the eighteenth-century statesman and writer Lord Chesterfield. Yet Lascelles remained single until he was thirty-nine. When and where he first met Princess Mary, the quiet, country-loving daughter of King George and Queen Mary, is not recorded, but his father's closeness to the court would have furnished a number of opportunities. They had certainly encountered each other at house parties at Chatsworth and Bolton Abbey in the first years of peace, and Lascelles had been a house guest at Balmoral, Windsor and Sandringham. Princess Mary, so members of her household believed, formed such an attachment to the tall, fair-moustached Harry Lascelles that 'had she not been able to have him, she would have remained unmarried', as one recalled sixty years later.

Somehow a myth has gained currency among the inter-war generation that Princess Mary was hard to marry off. Since she was only twenty-one when the war ended, this theory has little credibility, except that the stock of eligible husbands had dwindled considerably with the total unacceptability of any of the German princelings. There were still the Scandinavian royal houses, but it was 'tacitly agreed between the King and Queen', as James Pope-Hennessy recounted in his biography of Queen Mary, 'that they could not object should any of their children look to members of the English or Scottish nobility. This was indeed likely enough to happen, since, save for the Prince of Wales, the children of King George and Queen Mary had had no experience of Continental life.' One former retainer of the Princess Royal, who maintains firmly that it was a genuine love match, recalls the king and queen throwing two large receptions at Buckingham Palace with the understood aim of interesting the Princess in a potential suitor. The Earl of Sefton's heir, Viscount Molyneux, and Lord Dalkeith, heir to the Duke of Buccleuch, were in the first party; Lascelles in what might be called the second team. Queen Mary's diary records that in November 1921, Viscount Lascelles was staying at York Cottage on the Sandringham estate and that it was in a room of this small house that he proposed and was accepted. The Queen's entry for 20 November read: 'Went the usual rounds in the afternoon. At 6.30 Mary came to my room to announce to me her engagement to Lord Lascelles! We then told G. & then gave Harry L. our blessing. We had to keep it quiet owing to G. having to pass an order in council to give his consent. Of course everybody guessed what had happened & we were very cheerful & almost uproarious at dinner – We are delighted.' To her brother, the Marquess of Cambridge, the Queen wrote next day: 'We like him very much & it is such a blessing to feel she will not go abroad. *I* personally feel quite excited as you can imagine.' To a woman friend she wrote: 'Mary is radiant & I am getting *so* fond of him & we get on very well.' The engagement was announced publicly on 23 November and next day the queen took the couple driving in an open carriage through London, where, she noted, 'people seemed pleased to see them'. That afternoon,

Harry Lascelles was formally presented as a member of the family to the Queen Mother, Alexandra, at the Palace and, Queen Mary recorded in her diary, 'We had a most hilarious tea.'

The queen's apparent relief that her daughter would not be forced into some Continental match – though none seems to have been in evidence – was echoed in Mary's own somewhat plaintive message to the nation on the announcement of her betrothal: 'It is a great happiness to me that I am to remain in my native land and that my life will be spent among my own people.' The wedding itself, for the first of the sovereign's children to marry, was solemnized by the Archbishop of Canterbury in Westminster Abbey on 28 February 1922. It provided the first real splash of pageantry London had enjoyed since the coronation of 1911 and came as a welcome excuse to fling away the last vestiges of post-war malaise. Although Princess Mary was nothing like so much in the public eye as the dashing Prince of Wales, the Empire's most eligible bachelor, the wedding excited a genuine uprush of popular enthusiasm. It rather surprised her younger brother, the Duke of York (later King George VI), who wrote to the Prince of Wales, on a tour of India, 'Mary's wedding is causing a great deal of work to many people, & as far as I can make out the 28th is going to be a day of national rejoicing in every conceivable & unconceivable manner. . . . In fact it is now no longer Mary's wedding but (this from the papers) it is the "Abbey Wedding" or the "Royal Wedding" or the "National Wedding" or even the "People's Wedding" (I have heard it called) "of our beloved Princess".'

The wedding day turned out unseasonably sunny and warm and enormous crowds jostled for a view along the processional route. The Duke of York wrote to his brother, absent on his imperial progress, that 'everything was arranged wonderfully well. . . . Mary looked lovely in her wedding dress & was perfectly calm all through the ceremony.' In the afternoon, the queen gave a party at St James's Palace for what the *Yorkshire Post* called 'all branches of society' – including tenants from the king's and Lord Harewood's estates. (The earl had been made a Knight Grand Commander of the Royal Victorian Order on the eve of the wedding in honour of the family link; he was the first English nobleman for four hundred years to be the father-in-law of the daughter of a reigning king.) The wedding luncheon for 170 guests, the tables decorated with sweet peas and roses, was held in the State Banqueting Room of Buckingham Palace, with the overflow accommodated in the

State Ball Supper Room. At 3.45, bride and groom left for Paddington Station to begin a honeymoon in Shropshire and Italy; King George, the Queen reported, broke down as the couple left, pelted by paper horse-shoes and rose petals – 'I mercifully managed to keep up as I so much feared Mary wld break down. However, she was very brave & smiled away as they drove off in triumph to the station.' Along the route, hawkers shouted their souvenir wares: ' 'Arry and Mary and the wed-din' bell! Sixpence each!'

When they returned in the Yorkshire spring to take up residence at Goldsborough, Daniel Lascelles's Jacobean manor near Knares-borough – an event which caused unusual activity among the Harewood estate carpenters, who were kept busy making packing cases for the removals – their Rolls-Royce was ceremonially pulled on ropes up the mile-long drive by the young sons of estate workers. But the signs were already unmistakable that ownership of England would never again be as it was in 1914.

7

'England is Changing Hands'

The first full year of peace, so long awaited, turned out to be a disastrous one for the landed classes of England. In March of 1919, Lloyd George introduced a budget that, on top of the severe wartime increases in the rate of income tax, doubled death duties on estates worth over £2 million. The rate went from 20 to 40 per cent, with a graduated scale below that starting at 30 per cent on estates of £1 million. Henceforth too, land was to be valued for death duties at its current selling price rather than on the basis of existing rents, as had been the practice. The break-up of the great landed estates had begun before the war, in the wake of an earlier Lloyd George budget bearing heavily on the propertied classes – between 1910 and 1913 several hundred thousand acres changed hands – but the war itself was the last straw for many old families, with the new taxes following hard on the death of the heir in battle. It was not uncommon in the circumstances of the time for fathers and sons to die within a short period of each other, and even before the 1919 budget land was coming onto the market in an ever-increasing flow. By the end of March 1919, more than half a million acres were up for sale.

Under the headline 'Death Duties . . . the Old Order Doomed', *The Times* in May published a letter from the Duke of Marlborough contending that the aim of the new tax was 'social and political rather than financial'. Quoting the estimated yield from death duties that year, a mere £33.5 million out of a total anticipated revenue of £1,201,100,000, the Duke wrote from Blenheim that it was clear that the transmission of monetary power from father to son had become 'obnoxious to democratic opinion', and that this also applied to those whose wealth was tied up in great houses and estates. 'These fortresses of territorial influence it is proposed to raze in the name of social equality. . . . Are these historic houses, the abiding memorials of events which live in the hearts of Englishmen, to be converted into museums, bare relics of a dead past?' A tax which, as the duke put it, 'sequestrates nearly half of the whole', must, he thought, 'make it impossible for the heirs of those men to carry on the tradition.'

The Duke of Marlborough was not alone among his peers in feeling uneasy at the new temper in the land. A few months earlier, the Marquess of Northampton had written to *The Times* that 'landowning on a large scale is now generally felt to be a monopoly and is consequently unpopular.' The landowners of England could be forgiven for thinking that their Conservative friends in the coalition government had deserted them in their hour of need. What in fact was happening, as the *Estates Gazette* perceived in March 1919, was 'a revolution in landowning'. Most of the land going up for sale was being bought by its tenant farmers; tenants normally would be given first refusal, although speculators were busy and many formed syndicates to buy land for resale at a profit.

A new phrase began to gain widespread currency: 'England is changing hands'. Probably the inspiration of an advertising copywriter, it had by May 1920 reached the editorial columns of *The Times*, where an anonymous correspondent on the court circular page wrote on 19 May, 'We all know it now . . . England is changing hands.' Lamenting the loss of a way of life which for generations had been intimately involved with the land and its community, the writer saw the trend as 'a minor consequent tragedy of all we have gone through. . . . The old people, knowing there is no son or near relative left to keep up the old traditions, or so crippled by necessary taxation that they know "the boy" will never be able to carry on when they are gone, take the irrevocable step; the obliging agent appears, deferential, sympathetic, yet businesslike.'

The agents were certainly doing booming business. One firm alone announced 750,000 acres for sale during 1919, and in a few summer weeks more than two million acres were offered in *The Times* estate pages. The following year saw even more land coming onto the market: the Duke of Rutland sold 28,000 acres, about half of his Belvoir estate, for £1.5 million, subsequently putting 12,500 acres of Leicestershire up for sale for £1 million. The Duke of Beaufort and the Marquess of Bath were among other vendors. At the end of 1921 the *Estates Gazette* worked out that about one-quarter of England had changed hands, and that only included the sales which were reported in the national press – many were not. Altogether, it has been calculated that from 1918 to the end of 1921 between six and eight million acres changed ownership, the largest such permanent transfer, says one historian, since the dissolution of the monasteries.

The fifth Earl of Harewood was an early vendor in the great land sale. In June 1919, in reply to an appeal from his tenants, he composed an open letter to them from his London home at 13 Upper Belgrave Street, explaining why he felt it necessary to put some 10,000 acres of his North Riding estates on the market; the first time the family lands had been substantially broken up. Explaining that he was taxed, 'both income tax and super tax', on the gross rents he received, 45 per cent of which were earmarked to cover essential outgoings on the estate, he wrote: 'I am faced with the alternative of either reducing the "outgoings" substantially . . . or of having to leave the home where I have lived for so many years, and probably leave this country, for I have no other available home, nor if I had, would I make any other home in Yorkshire at my time of life. . . . The financial legislation since 1910 has been directed towards the breaking-up of the large landed estates. Mr. Lloyd George is in possession of full details as to the proportion of outgoings to gross rents on my estates, for I furnished them myself at his request some years ago, and I know other large landed proprietors did the same. . . . It is with infinite sorrow and regret that I have come to the decision to part with the oldest portion of my family property. . . . My only consolation is that the necessity has not arisen from any folly or extravagance of my own.'

In Harewood's case, of course, death duties were long past and played no part in his decision to sell, even if the general level of taxation did. Of forty titled landowners who put their acres on the market in the first half of 1919, only six had recently become liable for death duties. The rest were simply being prudent in slimming down unprofitable estates. Before 1914, estate expenditure had generally been reckoned to take about 35 per cent of gross rents, compared with Harewood's figure of 45 per cent in 1919; in the 1930s it was to go 70 per cent higher and the personal income of most landowners was down to half the pre-1914 level. Their financial position as a result of the land sales, says the historian F.M.L. Thompson (*English Landed Society in the Nineteenth Century*), became 'probably much healthier than . . . for many years'.

Selling went on, though at a less hectic pace, until the mid-1920s, but land prices fell with the repeal of the wartime legislation guaranteeing grain prices. The average selling price, at its peak £35 an acre, was down to a mere £11 an acre by 1929. The new owners of England, meanwhile, quite often found themselves worse off paying a mortgage than they had been when paying rent; in the 1930s it was said that half of Norfolk was owned by the banks.

The total paid for the Harewood acres, with 1326 remaining unsold, was a shade under a quarter of a million pounds, and the bulk of the land went to the tenants to whom Lord Harewood had promised first refusal. At the same time the earl was considering another option against the onslaught of the Inland Revenue: turning the rest of his estates into a company, either limited or unlimited, as a number of other owners had already done. His solicitors warned him of the necessity for any such change to be demonstrably bona fide and that there would be inconveniences, such as the obligation to hold regular directors' meetings. He did not finally make the transition until 1928, when the estates were formed into a limited company under the name of Harelles Trust Ltd, with the earl and his heir, Viscount Lascelles, as directors and a registered capital of £2000. The stated purpose of the business was 'the management and administration of landed property'. On the fifth earl's death in 1929 the Harewood estates, regarded as among the best managed in England, totalled 27,000 acres in Yorkshire and elsewhere.

Estate duty was eventually assessed at a modest £95,000. The fifth earl's various bequests included the leasehold of his London house, his horses, carriages and motors to his wife, along with £10,000 and the proceeds of the sale of his racehorses and brood mares. A full-size fire engine, one of his most cherished possessions, was a surprising item in the inventory of Harewood House left to the heir, Harry Lascelles; Edward, the younger son, inherited the sugar plantations in Barbados, in trust for himself and his male heirs. (Today, the West Indies estates have all been sold: Viscount Lascelles, heir to Lord Harewood, says with amusement that the only connection left is 'a lot of people called Lascelles or Harewood – there is even a Lascelles marmalade'.) Small bequests included £100 and a cottage in Hampshire to the earl's water bailiff, Henry Hutches, and £100 each to his coachman, his stud groom and each indoor servant who had been employed for ten years or more.

It was a microcosm of a life that was, almost imperceptibly, slipping away as *The Times* columnist had prophesied ten years before, though Harewood was slower than many English villages to lose the structured certainties of pre-1914 society. Unlike, for instance, the East Anglian villages so vividly embodied in Ronald Blythe's *Akenfield*, it did not lose its young men from the farms after a war which, harsh as it was, widened their horizons and taught them that easier livings were to be made in the factories and salerooms of the towns. The good, rich agricultural land of Wharfedale, easier to work than the heavy clay of Suffolk and Essex, drew the men back – that, and the congenial cosiness of a still-feudal community. John Bryant, in 1980 older than the century and the oldest inhabitant in Harewood village, a farm worker all his life who had 'never slept away from home' before he joined the Machine Gun Corps in the First World War, said most of the farm men were happy to come back after the Armistice.

The war itself, as in most rural communities in England, scarcely made its physical presence felt in Harewood. A Zeppelin unloaded a bomb over Lord Harewood's park and one on the Avenue, leaving three large dark brown patches on the road. Some windows were blown in at the nearby village of Collingham, where anti-aircraft guns and searchlights were set up. Derek Deakin's family has lived in Harewood since the early 1900s and owned the first – and still the only – petrol station in the village. He remembers his father, then a blacksmith by trade, working through the night in the Great War making rush orders of twelve sets of shoes at a time for the war horses which were stabled behind the Harewood Arms during their periods of rest from front-line duty. In January 1915, Lord Harewood, who was president of the West Riding Territorial Association, turned Harewood House into an auxiliary hospital for officers – it would serve the same function in the Second World War. The house at first accommodated thirty patients, later expanded to forty-nine, who stayed for periods ranging from two weeks to four months. A qualified matron was in charge of the hospital, but Lady Florence held the honorary rank of commandant.

The war left its indelible mark however; not only in those men who failed to return from the Western Front but in the irrevocable changes it wrought in the lives of those who, like John Bryant, had seen nothing of the world outside Wharfedale before being pitchforked into the army in a foreign land. Placid country ways which had scarcely changed in five centuries were unlikely to survive after 1918; young men whose greatest excitement had been a visit by horse-drawn charabanc to Leeds for an evening at the City Varieties would henceforth be restless at horizons bounded by the village pub and cricket pitch. Before the war, recalled John Bryant's younger brother Alfie, there had been two football teams and two cricket teams in Harewood; afterwards, interest in village sport and community activities began to wane as 'folks started knocking about more'.

Physically, Harewood in the early twenties still looked much like its Edwardian self. It was still mainly horses which used the untarmaced road, which was made of compacted round stones between high grass verges, and there was so little traffic of any kind that the village boys used to play marbles down the middle. There was a dirt yard in front of the Harewood Arms where the horse-drawn traps and carts pulled in, and the inn's landlord operated his own twice-daily charabanc service to the outskirts of Leeds, leaving at nine or ten in the morning and three or four in the afternoon. It took three-quarters of an hour for the two horses to pull the 'chara' to Moortown, four miles away, and from there you could get a penny tram into Leeds. A seat in the 'gods' at the City Varieties – still used as the setting for BBC Television's 'Good Old Days' music-hall programme – and a big fish and chip dinner, plus the tram fare, would still leave change out of a shilling. The first motor bus cost 1s. 3d. return to Leeds and the village boys used to watch for the Sunday arrival from Harrogate of the first motor car to be seen in Harewood, a dashing red vehicle driven by a man they nicknamed 'Daredevil Dick'. Mr Hawkins's covered wagon went every week to Leeds station taking vegetables, chickens and clean linen for the Harewoods' London home, and collecting their dirty laundry off the London train. The doctor still, in the early twenties, used to make his visits on horseback if the route lay across country, or by a smart horse and trap. Before the Harrogate road was metalled for motor traffic, a horse-drawn coach used to make the journey every Thursday, still sounding the traditional post horn. Farm labourers would walk cattle to the market at Otley, eight miles away, and walk home again after the sale, a journey of two and a half hours each way. It was not regarded as a hardship when there was no alternative. Neither was the grinding physical labour, literally from dawn till dusk, of the average agricultural worker. Life was work, and nothing but work, and this was not questioned or resented; you worked around eighteen hours a day and when you came home, as one old farm-worker with a deeply seamed face recalled, it was just 'a wash, summat to eat and up to bed, and then you didn't know any more until someone banged on your door next morning. You worked beyond your strength but you didn't know it.' He looked puzzled when asked what people then did for pleasure. 'Pleasure? You got your pleasure out of looking after the animals and doing up the horses and the harness well, doing things well.' There was no division between work and leisure: 'Now all you hear is people saying how many years they've got to do before they retire.'

By the time he was eight years old, this lad was put to work by his father, feeding hens and collecting eggs. At twelve, he was dispatched with the horse and cart to collect a load of coal from the nearest railway station. 'When I was thirteen,' he said proudly over a pint in the Harewood Arms, 'I could do anything a man could do – lamb a sheep, work a dog and work with cattle and horses.' Another pensioned farm-worker, Cliff Lancaster, who served the Harewood estate for twenty-seven years, was also put to work by his father in the First World War. Aged thirteen, he was paid 6d. a week 'and my tea' to feed the cattle, eventually progressing to a yearly payment of £8 'and my meat'.

There was a curious system by which you could elect how to be paid from this munificent sum. 'You could draw your pay during the year but I never did – if you'd drawn it, you hadn't it at the finish. I never smoked nor drank. You'd buy your clothes at year-end when you drew your pay. There were nothing much to spend money on – it were all village life then.' Agricultural wages went down steeply after the First World War, from £1 a week to 12s. 6d. and keep. Of necessity, the village community displayed a cooperative closeness: it was what today's sociological jargon would describe as a 'caring society', the warmth of which is still missed, with the harsh exigencies that brought it about blurred by time. Alfie Bryant remembers how the butcher would slap down a pound of sausages on top of a piece of pork belly (4d. a pound) to fill out a meal for some poor family. When farmers killed a bacon pig there was a custom of giving away 'the fry' – the liver and offal – always with the insistence that the dish be returned unwashed, otherwise bad luck would follow and 'the pig wouldn't take the salt' in the curing. 'If you was poorly, folks'd allus help,' said Alfie, who remembered one occasion when a woman who couldn't feed her new-born baby was told heartily by a neighbour to 'send the bairn down – I've enough milk to suck two.'

Clothes were handed down from child to child, carefully mended. The old villagers express astonished disapproval at the 'good stuff' sent to jumble sales today, and amazement that both buyers and sellers arrive in cars. The fact of a luxury such as motor transport becoming commonplace over their lifetime is somehow more easily accepted than the persistence of jumble sales, a poor society's custom, among the affluent middle-class commuters of West Yorkshire.

The big house and its family were always a presence in Harewood life, which still revolved around it in the years between the wars. If you lived in Harewood and did not work for one of the farmers in the area, you were almost certainly employed by the Lascelles as a forestry worker, estate labourer, farm-worker, gamekeeper, stud groom, chauffeur or domestic servant. To some extent the seasons in the village and the passage of the weeks were marked by the comings and goings of Lascelles and their house guests and the elaborate logistics of shuttling laundry, garden produce, personal belongings and people between Harewood and London. The fifth earl maintained his home in Belgravia and his son and Princess Mary still had the most gracious of town residences in Chesterfield House, Mayfair. In 1932, however, the new earl put up some of the contents for auction by Sotheby's and sold the house, which was demolished five years later to make way for a block of flats. The ten-storey, late-thirties building put up in its place still bears the name Chesterfield House. The Harewoods meanwhile moved to more modest premises in Green Street.

On the death of the fifth earl in 1929 his heir and Princess Mary – she was not given the title of Princess Royal by George V until 1932 – moved out of their rambling Jacobean manor at Goldsborough and into Harewood House, where they found the Victorian comforts, so impressive in Sir Charles Barry's day, had become distinctly threadbare. The Harewoods began a series of modernization schemes, starting with a partial rewiring of the house; there were not enough table lamps, the Princess discovered, and the voltage was different from that of Goldsborough, only ten miles away. In December 1929 the Yorkshire Electric Power Company quoted for installing electrical cooking equipment to replace the open coal grates which were still in use in the kitchen and still room. The equipment, available either in 'mottled enamel' at a cost of £805 16s. 6d. or stove black finish at £665 11s. 6d., would be capable, said the company, of catering for up to 150 people, though the number normally resident was between fifty and sixty at the most.

Sir Herbert Baker, the distinguished architect who had worked with Sir Edwin Lutyens on designing New Delhi, was called in to make the alterations needed to the interior, together with Brierley and Rutherford, the York architects who had succeeded John Carr's company and who still possessed the original plans for the house. These were found to be inaccurate and Baker had to redraw them, but with the minimum of disturbance to Barry's 1857 remodelling, he put in nine bathrooms and an oil central-heating system, improved the mid-Victorian lift mechanism and generally made the family quarters on the eastern side of the house more convenient and habitable. He also created a dressing room for the princess on the ground floor, between the East Bedroom, which Edwin Lascelles had designed for his own use, and the former study adjoining the old Library, which was remodelled in the 1960s to become the China Room. Baker was careful to retain the essential Adam character, including a fireplace flanked by glass-fronted cases which now contain the present earl's collection of jade, amber and quartz.

The cost of the conversion work mounted alarmingly, a repetition for the sixth earl of his great-grandfather's experience with Barry. The total bills came to more than £44,000, of which building work accounted for £18,000 including the lift installation, and plumbing alterations £10,800. A London firm of sanitary engineers called Dent and Hellyer of Red Lion Square had been contracted to carry out the plumbing work, and in the summer of 1932 they were complaining of dilatory payment and requesting 'a substantial amount on account without any further delay'. Through the architects, Lord Harewood's agent N.H.T. FitzRoy queried the size of the bills and was told they were due to the peculiarly taxing conditions of working in the house with its circuitous routes and narrow passages. Apart from new drains, Dent and Hellyer had had to install two miles of lead, copper and iron piping, and thousands of bends, valves, and screwed and soldered joints. In many cases, Brierley and Rutherford wrote in a lengthy letter to Mr FitzRoy, the piping had to be bent experimentally for two or three trial fittings. 'The drainage had to be laid in the underground ducts under the most horrible and difficult conditions and not many firms could have supplied men who would have stuck to such a beastly job as Dent and Hellyer's did,' the firm explained in unusually heartfelt terms. But the architects agreed to reduce by £150 their own outstanding balance of £950 on total fees of £2500.

Sir Herbert Baker would have liked to see the exterior stonework cleaned of its coating of industrial grime – millstone grit, as one can see from the public buildings of many Northern Victorian cities, has a special propensity for attracting an even layer of soot; in extreme cases, it takes on the depth and sheen of black basalt or jet. 'My experience of black countries,' Baker remarked in a letter, '[is] that the better the stone, the blacker it gets; the reason being that the surface of bad stone wears off in the same way that plane trees cast their dirty bark and look clean in London.' The south and west elevations of Harewood were much dirtier than the north front – a common experience, according to other local landowners, up to the Clean Air Acts of the 1950s: pollution was carried over the Pennines from Bradford and Halifax by the prevailing winds and dumped in Wharfedale. At one time Otley was reputed to have the highest concentration of soot in the county. But Baker correctly assumed that Lord Harewood would not want to take on this extra cost, and in fact the external stonework was not cleaned until 1972.

Having brought some modern standards of warmth, comfort and convenience to the Carr and Adam mansion, the new earl and countess had considerable contributions to make to the already renowned Harewood collection. Harry Lascelles's inspired collecting had yielded a particularly rich harvest of Italian paintings from the fifteenth and early sixteenth centuries, and these were now moved in from Goldsborough, while Princess Mary had a passion for miniature ornaments and semi-precious carved stones. Lord Harewood had a talent for embroidery – shared even now by some Yorkshire squires, perhaps a legacy of long, pre-television winter evenings when the wind howled down from the dales – and he made petit point tapestry covers to replace the threadbare seats of four Chippendale chairs in the Gallery. Restoration was carried out on other Chippendale pieces and later on the Victorian Billiard Room, which was not in keeping with the austerely elegant style of the original house, was converted into the Rose Drawing Room.

In some rooms it was impossible to disentangle the Victorian character from the original – the Dining Room, Mary Mauchline commented, had become 'irredeemable' – but over the ten years which it took to complete the translation from Goldsborough, the essential eighteenth-century house gradually re-emerged from under the florid taste of the Victorian squirearchy. The Italian Renaissance paintings, not least the two Bellinis of Madonna subjects which were brought over from the Goldsborough dining room, gave a new and richer character to the interior of the house, and some long-missing elements were also restored, including some early English watercolours of Harewood which had been sold by the fourth earl at Christie's in 1858. The best known of these was Turner's *Distant View of the South Front of Harewood House*, painted for Edward, Viscount Lascelles, in 1798. It had been in the possession of a Lascelles aunt, the Countess of Wharncliffe, who gave it to Harry Lascelles as a wedding present in 1922. Now it returned to hang in its rightful home, along with the other great topographical watercolours of the house and its surrounding landscape by Turner and Girtin.

Goldsborough Hall remained in the family until 1939, eventually being sold to become a school. The move proceeded in leisurely fashion, with domestic concerns taking priority. Princess Mary supervised the transfer of her personal possessions with typical thoroughness and attention to detail, listing her instructions to the packers down to minor items of nursery furniture which were required for the two junior Lascelles, George and Gerald, then aged six and five. A hand-written memorandum dated 27 November 1930 to the housekeeper has survived among the Harewood papers: 'When the furniture van collects the various things, I want the rocking-horse, also the low round table from the Day Nursery and the glass medicine cupboard from the night nursery. Will you please send all the clothes baskets from the visitors' rooms and his Lordship's also from the nursery.' As the shooting season of 1930 approached, she also asked for 'all the small blue napkins for our luncheon case' to be sent over to Harewood, together with the 'washable linings for plate, glasses, etc. for ditto.'

The stately round of a country-house year proceeded on its course largely uninterrupted by the modernization work and the movement of furniture vans. The name of Sir Herbert Baker, the architect in charge, was the first to be recorded in the second Harewood visitors' book which opened in 1930; the first, a small brown leather-bound volume, well rubbed with use, had spanned the years 1896 to 1929. Baker was to be a frequent guest, and there were, naturally, many royal entries. 'Albert' and 'Elizabeth' came for three days in early December 1931 – the Duke and Duchess of York, who six years later were to become King George VI and Queen Elizabeth. The king and queen themselves came in August 1932, heading a large house party of about two dozen including a bevy of equerries and aides-de-camp. Other regular royal visitors in the thirties included Princess Alice, Countess of Athlone, and her tall, imposing-looking husband, Queen Mary's brother; Lady Patricia Ramsay and the Prince of Wales, signing the book in a bold, extrovert hand in December 1933. Queen Mary, with or without the king, made a point of spending a week of August at Harewood each year on her way north to Balmoral. The Princess Royal was particular about keeping up her visitors' book, inserting slips later on where forgetful visitors had left without signing. Among other visitors in those inter-war years were Sir Cosmo Duff Gordon, who had (not without considerable social embarrassment) been one of the few male passengers saved from the sinking Titanic in 1912, the 'Yellow Earl' of Lonsdale, the Duke of Wellington's heir, Gerald Wellesley, the architect Reginald Blomfield and the Archbishop of Canterbury, Cosmo Gordon Lang, who spent a couple of days there in the summer of 1936 before the Abdication crisis broke over his head.

The household virtually moved to London at the end of April and returned in August. Teddy Salmon, who had joined the service of Lord Lascelles in 1925 as second chauffeur for £2 a week plus food allowance, recalled that it was then 'the best part of a day's work' to drive down to London. The Princess often travelled by train while the car followed; they had two Rolls-Royces, a big 40/50 limousine and the smaller 20/25 saloon, handier for town. The staff would pack into a Dennis shooting brake which held about six people; the butler, cook and footman would move to London for the season, while other staff remained behind to do the spring cleaning and 'leave everything sheeted up' until the family's return. The family ties of the staff never interfered with the logistics of domestic service: Salmon would leave his wife in their cottage at Harewood during the season, travelling back by train to see her when he had a free weekend. Long separations, cancelled holidays, broken dates for the unmarried, were all part of the accepted pattern of life below stairs. It was accepted, if reluctantly, as part of the price of an otherwise protected, even cosy livelihood which, as well as providing security while the dole queues were lengthening all over Britain, offered a snug family association with their employers which did much, even in retrospect, to soften the casual treatment of their own lives.

Of the two broad classes of employee on a big country estate, the personal domestic servants such as valets and ladies' maids had an easier physical existence, often with plenty of rest time during the day, and a more interesting life, lived vicariously through their lords and ladies, but they gave up the independence which, for all the hard manual grind, was enjoyed by household and estate workers not tied by the erratic exigencies of personal service. When Joe Groom, the appropriately named Valet Groom of the Chambers to the sixth earl and the Princess Royal, drove from Harewood to London in a small car after the princess's death in 1965, he remarked to Teddy Salmon at the wheel how different the view of the road was from that in the tall old Rolls. 'Aye,' said Salmon drily, 'you're not the lord of the manor now.'

Groom, like many personal servants, never married, maintaining friendships in his seventies – often at long distance – with others of his kind like the Princess Royal's old ladies' maids. Reminiscing in his neatly kept, rent-free cottage in the Square at Harewood, surrounded by silver-framed photographs and memorabilia of his late employers, Groom said simply: 'You gave your life to them.' For most, there was no question of marrying: 'We never had the time. We used to have a saying, "when a donkey dies, a lady's maid marries" – and you know how long donkeys live.' Groom, a small cheerful man, chuckled, but the story he proceeded to tell of one lady's maid called Williams (they often never even knew one another's Christian names) was quietly appalling in the vision it conjured up of wasted years and dried-up affections. Williams, a remarkable beauty among her peers, had had two or three serious admirers but she worked for a very grand duchess who, having given her an evening off, would often at the last moment and with formidable charm, say, 'I'm sorry, Williams, but I'm going to need you after all. . . .' Someone would be dispatched with a message to the waiting boyfriend; 'of course in the end they gave up,' said Groom. In old age, Miss Williams confessed to regret at her lost chances; yet at the time, and perhaps even now, it would never have occurred to her to refuse to subordinate her personal life whenever required to that of her employer. Groom related the sad little tale with his customary sunny demeanour; his own regrets, whatever they may be, have been tucked away in the drawers of his mind as tidily as the clothes he once folded for Lord Harewood.

Groom joined the Harewood household from valeting for the Earl of Denbigh in 1939, shortly before the outbreak of war. A Cheshire-born man, he had started in service as hallboy in the house of a Derbyshire baronet, graduated to footman and thence, as often happened, to valet. Footmen were frequently detailed by the butler to 'unpack for' male weekend guests who had not brought their own valets, and housemaids would be instructed by the head housekeeper to do the same for maidless lady guests. The phrase 'unpack for' meant that that servant was supposed to look after that particular guest's clothes and needs for the whole weekend; valeting experience was thus gained which could be used to move up into that field if one did not aspire to the hierarchic eminence of butler or head housekeeper.

Groom's duties for the Harewoods were relatively light; apart from valeting the Earl's clothes, he had to replenish the writing desks scattered about the Princess Royal's homes – fill the inkpots with red and blue ink, sharpen a selection of red, black and blue pencils, and check that the filled water-bottle and brush were placed ready for sealing the letters – royalty was not expected to lick envelope flaps. The princess was an inveterate correspondent, even using the time on a train journey to write letters on a travelling pad, and there were always four or five letters for each morning and afternoon post.

Groom had his own quarters and at Harewood House these consisted of a comfortable suite of bedroom and sitting room. There were often several hours free in the middle of the day and after laying out the evening clothes, if those were required. He was engaged at £5 a month and wore the customary valets' 'uniform' of clerical grey suit with waistcoat, stiffly starched collar and discreet tie. After waking the earl with tea at 7.50 a.m. and switching on the wireless for morning prayers, he would lay out the day's selected suit, put out a fresh shirt and swing out the tie rack. He never took a suit to the dry cleaner's: 'If they are looked after properly they don't need it.' Suits, of course, came in multiples in such households; three shooting suits would be packed for a short trip to the moors. They were always folded away in tallboys, not hung in wardrobes: 'If you fold a jacket properly, it never creases.'

The sixth earl, like his ancestors, was a countryman by taste and instinct. At Goldsborough in the twenties he had reared one of England's best Guernsey herds and in 1923 became president of the Guernsey Cattle Society. Once married to the king's daughter, however, he inevitably had to spend more time in London than he would have liked, though the princess too was happiest among her flowers and shrubs in Yorkshire, pottering round the gardens in the decrepit old hat her maid called 'that museum piece'. She used to say that she never felt properly in the country until she reached Harewood. In late middle age, they were a quiet, retiring couple; when the diary permitted a free evening in London, it was spent at home rather than at the theatre or opera, the princess doing needlework or knitting, and the earl, who had a passion for jigsaws to the extent of joining a hobbyists' club, poring over a complex puzzle.

When war broke out again in September 1939, the painstaking restoration of Harewood House during the thirties had only just been completed. Once again it reverted to its 1914–18 role as an officers' hospital. The Gallery became a ward of thirty beds, its paintings left on the walls but protected by thick sheets of hardboard. Many of the house treasures were moved down to the cavernous 'sub-hall' under the entrance lobby, where the tall cream-painted columns were cased in. Later on in the war, sixteen German and Italian prisoners-of-war were billeted on the estate, their labour divided among the different departments. By 1943 most of the south park was ploughed up for corn and Cliff Lancaster recalled an incident when the Italians stopped stooking the corn in front of the house in protest because some of the officers were taking photographs from the bedroom windows; they complained that these would be used as 'propaganda'.

When Lancaster joined the estate as a horseman in 1941 he earned £2 8s. a week and the only holidays the farm workers had were Christmas Day, Easter Sunday and Saturday afternoons. But on 4 June 1941, a never-to-be-forgotten day, Lord Harewood sent round a note with the pay to say that from then on there would be one week's paid holiday a year, plus a quarter of an hour's 'bait time' for breakfast between 9 and 9.15 a.m. The farm then grew corn and root vegetables and furnished the dairy produce for the hospital and the Harewoods' own kitchen. Fields growing carrots and mangolds were set among the corn as firebreaks in case of bombs. In 1941 the farm as such occupied only thirty acres but so much land was ploughed up for grain that Lancaster remembered 'for two years after the war you could stand at Harewood House and see nothing but corn'. Lancaster presently became farm foreman, taking over from a man whose father had been foreman before him: 'There were people here then who had been on the estate for generations'. It was still a close-knit community, marrying within itself, 'brother and sister marrying brother and sister'. But this war was coming closer to home.

Both Lascelles sons were in the army, George in the family regiment, the Grenadier Guards, and Gerald in the Rifle Brigade. Both had joined as private soldiers and George had risen to the rank of captain when in June 1944 he was captured in Italy and eventually sent to the supposedly impregnable fortress of Colditz, along with other scions of the British aristocracy whom the Nazis, with their naive belief in the importance of such rank, intended to hold as special hostages. Lascelles spent his imprisonment studying music, laying the foundations in Colditz of his future career as an international authority on opera.

When he was repatriated on the evening of V-E Day, it was to a different England from the one he had known in 1939. The Second World War had taken a far greater physical toll than the first, not only in the blitzed hearts of the cities but in the threadbare shabbiness that had descended on the country, from the great, boarded-up mansions to the women in their drab 'Utility' clothes queueing at butchers' shops which displayed the chilling sign 'Horsemeat – For Human Consumption Only'. By the end of July, a Labour Government was massively in power, backed overwhelmingly by the service vote and bent on an ambitious programme of social reform at the same time as it struggled with the appalling tasks of reconstruction. Wartime bureaucracy lingered on, merely frustrating now that the driving purpose that made it tolerable had gone. The British were mortally tired and drained by six years of monumental, day-and-night anxiety; an immense weariness lay over the country from which it would, perhaps, never quite recover.

In the bitter winter of 1946–7, the old earl, whose health had weakened with the anxiety over his heir, seemed at last to improve. He and the Princess Royal went to Torquay on the mild south Devon coast for six weeks early in the new year, celebrating their silver wedding there on 22 February. They returned to Yorkshire in the middle of the worst blizzards of the century, and Lord Harewood developed bronchial trouble that turned to pneumonia. In May he died at Harewood House at the comparatively early age of sixty-five. George VI flew up to his brother-in-law's funeral on 28 May, wearing a black armband on his army uniform. Royal mourning was waived 'in view of the current difficulties in connection with clothes'. The funeral was two days after Queen Mary's eightieth birthday; she sent pink and white carnations from her birthday table 'in loving remembrance from a devoted mother-in-law'. The Princess Royal's wreath was of wild rhododendrons gathered from his favourite part of the garden and shaped into a huge cross bearing the inscription, 'In gratitude to God for twenty-five years of perfect love and companionship.' Both Lascelles sons were in army uniform for the simple ceremony at Harewood parish church; George, at twenty-four and still trying to adjust to peace after his prisoner-of-war experiences, had entered on his inheritance at probably the bleakest moment of modern times for the landed aristocracy.

8

A Taste for the Arts

At this point in its history Harewood was, ironically enough, richer in works of art than it had ever been, or ever would be again. Although they were still in storage from the war or – in the case of many of the paintings – concealed *in situ* behind protective panels of hardboard, the contents of the house had been greatly enriched by the sixth earl, whose knowledge and flair as a collector were unrivalled in the family since the time of Beau Lascelles, and who had created a collection of European art far superior to the family portraits, sporting paintings and topographical works found in most English country houses. A cascade of treasures had come his way through the romantic accident of the Clanricarde inheritance – mainly Italian, Flemish, Dutch and English paintings and a notable collection of gold snuffboxes – and his marriage into the royal family had provided further enrichment in the way of presents from royal in-laws and purchases by Queen Mary in her indefatigable rounds of the dealers. The Princess Royal also had an informed taste for paintings and shared her husband's enthusiasm for the pursuit of finds in the saleroom.

Both as Viscount Lascelles and the sixth Earl of Harewood, Harry Lascelles was the spiritual heir of the first viscount, Edward 'Beau' Lascelles, the bachelor collector, art patron and amateur painter who died in 1814 before he could succeed to the title. They were the only two in the family who added more than the statutory portraits or sporting pictures to the walls of Harewood House. Beau Lascelles' own portrait by John Hoppner, for which he paid £36 15s. in April 1797, reveals a plump, well-groomed young man in wine-coloured coat and white cravat, his hair lightly powdered in the fashion of the time, and with that certain resemblance to the Prince of Wales which so displeased 'Prinny' that he called Lascelles 'the Pretender'. He had something else in common with the prince in his taste for Sèvres porcelain, and the brilliant collection he assembled at the beginning of the nineteenth century became one of the most distinctive contributions to any English country house. It still ranks as one of the finest in England, although inroads were made with the sale of some pieces in the 1960s, and it is probably the finest outside that built up by the Prince Regent at Carlton House and the Royal Pavilion, Brighton (now housed at Buckingham Palace and Windsor Castle, and that in the Wallace Collection, founded by the third Marquess of Hertford.

All three collections were formed at roughly the same time, during the brief Peace of Amiens which followed the first Napoleonic Wars and which brought aristocratic English connoisseurs flocking across the Channel in search of prizes among the debris left by the French Revolution. The possessions of the French royal family and aristocracy were being dispersed at bargain prices in the salerooms of Paris and it was here that Beau Lascelles made most of his discoveries on a visit in 1802. Most of the Sèvres in all three collections – the Harewood, the Royal and the Wallace – is of such quality that experts consider the pieces must have come from the same source, probably one of the French royal palaces. It has been said that, as a result of these inspired collecting forays after the Revolution, Sèvres can be seen and studied better in England than in its country of origin.

For 150 years, however, the Harewood collection remained virtually unknown, even to historians of Sèvres, and it was only after the Second World War, when the seventh earl decided to open the house to the public, that the magnificent pieces appeared on view. To connoisseurs of porcelain, it was a revelation. A series of scholarly articles on the Harewood Sèvres published in *Apollo* magazine in 1964, 1965 and 1966 described the collection as possessing the major qualities of Sèvres – the figure scenes done with the richness and detail of an oil painting, the unsurpassed colour grounds, including the highly prized 'rose Pompadour' introduced in 1757, and the elaborate gilding work. The pieces at Harewood date from 1753, when Louis XV took a quarter share in the newly established Sèvres company that replaced the old manufactory at Vincennes, to 1793, a year later than any piece in the Windsor collection.

Beau Lascelles's preference was for the brilliantly enamelled porcelains produced at Sèvres, but he also bought examples of the plain biscuit figures and the whole collection, from its massive garnitures to small individual pieces, contains many rarities not even matched by the royal acquisitions. One of these is the magnificent three-foot-high clock in the Music Room, made in the workshop of the late eighteenth-century Paris clockmaker Nicolas Sotiau, possibly for Marie Antoinette. Its inset panels of painted Sèvres are said to be unmatched in their scale and quality. The 'Harewood Bottles', matched vases made between 1760 and 1775 and of a design apparently unique to this collection, are also outstanding. But the most splendid acquisition must be the tea service bearing the date 1779 which tradition says was given to Marie Antoinette by the City of Paris. In the opinion of Hugh Tait, the Sèvres expert whose *Apollo* articles furnish the most detailed account of the collection, it must 'undoubtedly rank as one of the most splendid ever produced at Sèvres'. Painting and thick gilding, he observed, had been lavished on it to an extent that led him to doubt whether it had ever been intended for use; it might simply have been conceived as a piece of decorative art. It had survived through the years, he noted, in 'marvellous condition'.

After his foray to Paris, during which he also found most of the Chinese mounted porcelain now to be seen at Harewood House, Beau Lascelles continued to build up his Sèvres collection through London dealers, and it was a taste evidently shared by his father, the first earl, whose account books for the years 1807 to 1812 are littered with entries for china, sometimes Sèvres, sometimes Oriental or not specified, purchased from the Bond Street firm of Robert Fogg. In 1810 he spent an astounding £1400 at Fogg's. The first earl also frequently bought inexpensive pieces of Wedgwood and 'dessert figures' from the Derby factory of William Duesbury II. In 1807 Beau Lascelles also patronized Mr Fogg's establishment, buying a quantity of Sèvres, including twelve dozen plates at eight guineas a dozen and a pair of 'Seve Tee Tureens' at fifteen guineas. The entire bill came to £600. By 1815, the year after Beau Lascelles's death, the Harewood porcelain collection was already famous enough for Queen Charlotte, the wife of George III, to make a special journey to Yorkshire to see it, accompanied by the Prince Regent.

Beau Lascelles, of whom a contemporary diarist noted: 'Young Mr. Lascelles has a taste for the arts, and has practised a little,' was also responsible, through his active patronage of rising young watercolour painters and his desire to perfect his own skills in that medium, for equipping the house with some of its most splendid topographical works by Turner, Girtin and Varley in the last years of the eighteenth century. His taste was inherited from his father Edward, though the elder Lascelles, the cavalry officer and country squire who came into his cousin Edwin's estate, does not seem to have been a serious collector. The first major works of art to appear in the newly built Harewood House were, not surprisingly, family portraits. Edwin Lascelles celebrated his new country house in traditional style by commissioning Sir Joshua Reynolds to paint him, full length, splendidly attired in a rose-purple coat and waistcoat trimmed with gold braid, plum-coloured breeches, white striped stockings, a walking stick elegantly posed in his right hand and a three-cornered hat tucked underneath his left arm. Harewood House, naturally, appeared in the background, seen in the distance under a sunset sky. Lascelles sat three times for the portrait, in June 1765, May 1766 and June 1768, and made three payments to Reynolds, each of £157 10s. Edwin's cousin Edward was also painted by Reynolds, long before his inheritance; his portrait was done between 1762 and 1764, three-quarter length in dashing, steel-blue Van Dyck dress with a lace collar and cuffs. When he gained his earldom in 1812, he immediately commissioned an artist to reflect his new status by changing the baron's robes in his earlier portrait by Hoppner.

The politically active second earl, Henry, was painted by Sir Thomas Lawrence before he succeeded to the title; again, Harewood House was part of the distant landscape behind the powerful figure in an ankle-length brown greatcoat, every inch the established man of affairs. The third earl, the outgoing personality who commissioned Sir Charles Barry to reconstruct the entire façade of Harewood in the 1840s, running himself into considerable financial stress in the process, was presented with a portrait of himself in 1848 by members of the Bramham Moor Hunt 'as a token of their gratitude to his father and himself for their kindness and liberality in keeping the hounds'; they had been kennelled at Harewood for twenty years because of the lack of interest in hunting by the current head of the Lane-Fox family of Bramham Park, founders of the hunt. The portrait was painted by the then president of the Royal Academy, Sir Francis Grant, and appropriately shows the earl as master of hounds, mounted on his hack Cinderella, with a background of moorland. Nine years after it was finished, he died in a hunting accident. In 1888 the fourth earl sat for his immortalization in paint by Sir Edward Poynter, a picture which breathes the essence of high

Victorian stability and prosperous assurance. But beyond these expected gestures to posterity – most of which can now be seen in the Dining Room at Harewood – little was added in the course of a century, until the advent of the Viscount Lascelles who became father of the present earl, and who combined his peacetime military career before the First World War with the cultivation of a connoissseur's eye in Europe's art galleries.

It was while serving as an honorary attaché to the Diplomatic Service in Rome in 1905–7 that Lascelles, then a captain in the Grenadier Guards reserve, began his serious collecting with purchases of eighteenth-century French paintings. But the means for acquiring major works did not come his way until 1916, when in the course of a special winter leave in London after being wounded in France, he had the kind of good fortune associated with folklore and fairy tales. Since 1845, the Lascelles family had been connected by marriage to that of the Marquesses of Clanricarde and through them to the British Prime Minister and statesman George Canning, whose daughter Harriet had married the first Marquess of Clanricarde. The second Marquess, Hubert de Burgh, was Harry Lascelles's great-uncle and a notoriously harsh Irish landlord. He was also one of the great eccentrics of Edwardian London. He dressed like a tramp, was reputed to scavenge for discarded sandwiches in the waste paper baskets of his clubs, where other members kept well clear of him, yet was an informed and discriminating collector who haunted the salerooms and art galleries of St James, often to the discomfiture of elegant young salesmen who did not know of his identity or considerable fortune. The family seat, Portumna Castle in County Galway, was filled with fine paintings of all the major European schools, which had been saved from destruction in a fire at the castle in 1826, and Lord Clanricarde, who was unmarried, had no direct heir.

Harry Lascelles rarely saw his eccentric and embarrassing relative, but that February day in 1916 their paths crossed in the St James's Club at 106 Piccadilly. Lascelles, so the family story goes, entered the club accompanied by a couple of Army friends. Spotting his great-uncle, he excused himself, saying that he must have a word with the old man, whom he had not seen for a long time. The old marquess, then eighty-three, was delighted to find that his great-nephew shared a taste for collecting. They talked long and enthusiastically about art and the pleasures of the chase in the saleroom. In due course, Lascelles rejoined his regiment in France, the afternoon in the St James's Club forgotten.

But the marquess returned to his London residence and rewrote his will. Two months later he died. Harry Lascelles was the principal beneficiary, inheriting a fortune of £2,500,000 and the art collection of the Clanricardes and Cannings. In his late thirties, and with a fine war record to his credit, he became at a stroke one of the richest and most eligible bachelors in Britain. In 1919 he commissioned a posthumous portrait of his benefactor by Sir Leslie Ward, better known as 'Spy' of the *Vanity Fair* cartoons. The marquess was painted full length, dressed all in black with a black hat and seated at a table holding one of his favourite snuffboxes.

In the autumn of 1919, Lascelles invested part of his new-found fortune in what was described by *The Times* as 'one of the finest town houses in existence' – Chesterfield House in Mayfair, built by Isaac Ware in the 1740s for the fourth Earl of Chesterfield and filled by him with exquisite marble statuary, French furniture and works of art. The house, which stood at the corner of South Audley Street and Curzon Street, facing down Great Stanhope Street (now Stanhope Gate) to the park, was famous for its magnificently decorated walls, which precluded many of the rooms from displaying pictures, but Chesterfield was determined none the less to fill as many rooms as he could with fine paintings. He acquired a unique series of literary portraits, from Shakespeare to his own contemporaries, and had them mounted in baroque stucco frames. In November 1748 he wrote to a friend for whom he had secured a diplomatic posting to The Hague: 'It is very likely that many good pictures of Rubens, Teniers and other Flemish and Dutch masters may be picked up now at reasonable rates. If so . . . I should be glad to profit of it as an humble dilettante. I have already, as you know, a most beautiful landscape by Rubens, and a pretty little piece by Teniers; but if you could meet with a large capital history or allegorical piece of Rubens, with the figures as big as the life, I would go pretty deep to have it, as also for a large and capital picture of Teniers.' The Rubens was quickly found, and a Teniers heard of, and before the end of that year Lord Chesterfield was writing to his friend in Holland: 'My great room will be as full of pictures as it ought to be; and all capital ones.'

The house, which had been let in 1849 to the Marquess of Abercorn for £3000 a year – the fifth Earl of Chesterfield being in financial difficulties at the time – was denuded of most of its contents when the seventh earl sold it in 1869. They were removed to the Chesterfields'

Derbyshire seat, Bretby, and by great good fortune many of them were coming up for sale there at the time Harry Lascelles bought the Mayfair mansion, so he was able to bring back many of the house's original contents, including the literary portraits. Lascelles also added his own finest and most recent acquisition to Chesterfield House – Titian's *Death of Actaeon*, which was given a whole wall of the dining room. The painting which was to cause such a storm when the Harewood trustees put it up for sale in 1971 had originally been in the Orleans Collection formed by the Regent of France in the first half of the eighteenth century and dispersed in English salerooms around 1800. Lascelles bought it from Earl Brownlow through Agnew's, the Bond Street dealers. He also hung many of the fine Clanricarde Dutch paintings in his London home, and two other treasures of his own finding: *St Jerome* by Cima da Conegliano and *A Night Scene* by El Greco, a work which, as one art historian wrote in 1922, 'once seen can never be forgotten, a creation of absolutely haunting power'. Both the latter are now in Harewood House, along with two exquisite Bellini paintings of the Madonna acquired by Lord Lascelles in London.

After his marriage to Princess Mary in February 1922, Chesterfield House became a centre of aristocratic young society and in 1932, when the Lascelles – by then Earl and Countess of Harewood – sold it for a smaller town house, most of the best works of art were taken to Harewood, some furniture being sold through Sotheby's. The royal wedding contributed in its own way to the Harewood collections: presents of paintings came from the king and queen, the Harewood tenants – who clubbed together to commission a portrait of the princess by Oswald Birley – the people of South Africa and Colnaghi's, the fine art dealers, among others. Sir John Lavery painted a view of the wedding procession along the Mall, seen from Carlton House Terrace; it now hangs in the room known as Lord Harewood's Sitting Room, along with Frank Salisbury's painting of Princess Mary signing the register in Westminster Abbey on 28 February 1922. A great-aunt, Lady Wenlock, did a charming pastel view of Florence seen from the Villa Medici at Fiesole, where the couple spent part of their honeymoon.

The twenties and thirties saw many purchases by the Lascelles, who became the sixth earl and countess in 1929. A catalogue of the Harewood collection, prepared in 1936, reveals the rich variety of art in the house during the time the Harewoods were restoring it, installing modern amenities, stripping away the fusty Victorian furnishings and

The sixth Earl of Harewood in garter robes,
by Sir William Nicholson

The Music Room

The Princess Royal's
Sitting Room

The Rose Drawing Room

The Green Drawing Room

The seventh Earl and Countess of Harewood

The Entrance Hall, with Epstein's *Adam*

Opposite above Chippendale library table,
sold from Harewood in 1965

Opposite below Titian: *The Death of Actaeon*,
sold by the Harewood trustees at Christie's in 1971
for a (then) record £1,680,000

Viscount Lascelles, heir to Harewood, with his wife

bringing it to a peak of elegant living which would last for only a few months before the precarious European peace collapsed in September 1939. There were eighty-four paintings of the Italian school, including the *Death of Actaeon*; thirty-six of the Flemish school; sixty-two of the Dutch School, almost all inherited from Lord Clanricarde; eighteen of the French school, three each of the Spanish and German schools and two hundred and ninety of the English school – forty-six of them from Clanricarde, fifty-three acquired by the sixth earl. Lord Harewood could pride himself on having retrieved several fine early topographical works connected with the house which had either been sold in the mid-nineteenth century or given to other branches of the family. Girtin's 1798 view of Harewood House and its park, for instance, painted under a stormy sunset and probably executed for Beau Lascelles, was sold at Christie's in May 1858, acquired by Lord Penrhyn and subsequently by Lady Louisa Egerton. It was regained by Lord Lascelles in 1919. Another Girtin of 1798, this time of Harewood Bridge, was in the same Christie's sale and was only bought back in 1931 by the Princess Royal. Both were featured in the 1934 exhibition of British art at Burlington House.

A more famous view of the house, Turner's watercolour of the south front, done also in 1798 for Beau Lascelles and kept at first in the family's London home, Harewood House in Hanover Square, was given by the fourth earl to his sister the Countess of Wharncliffe, who graciously returned it to her great-nephew as a wedding present in 1922. Along with Girtin's complementary view from the south west, it had been lent to Sir Thomas Lawrence in 1822 to provide him, it is thought, with data for the landscape background to his portrait of the second earl. The Turner was exhibited in the Palace of the Arts at the British Empire Exhibition at Wembley in 1924 and reproduced in the souvenir book. Also featured at the Wembley exhibition, under a section in the Palace of the Arts labelled 'Empire Builders', was a portrait of George Canning as a boy at Eton, one of Gainsborough's last works, and one of his son Charles, Earl Canning, by Sir George Hayter; both had come from the Clanricarde inheritance.

Two other sisters of the fourth earl, Lady Florence Cust and Lady Mary Meade, were given Turners of Harewood House, but they too returned to their proper home within a generation. The sixth earl found two Maltons of Harewood House, done in 1778, and traced several other family connections in the saleroom. In 1925, when he and Princess

Mary were living at the Jacobean Goldsborough Hall, between Harewood and Knaresborough, he discovered and bought at Christie's a portrait of Goldsborough's builder, Judge Hutton. Queen Mary, in one of her antique-hunting expeditions through the Lanes of Brighton in 1925, found a portrait of Harriet Canning, Marchioness of Clanricarde, drawn in 1855 by James Rannie Swinton, and she bought it for her son-in-law.

There were gifts of paintings between husband and wife, too: a George Stubbs study of a black pony and dog was given to the earl by Princess Mary in 1928. The feeling of family life which still gives Harewood the atmosphere of a home temporarily vacated by its owners is nowhere more evocative than in the two paintings by Ambrose McEvoy of the young Viscount Lascelles (the present earl) in 1926, aged three; the wooden parrot used in one of them as a prop sits today, somewhat battered by time, in front of the picture in Lord Harewood's Sitting Room.

Traditional English sporting pictures were not neglected: an Alfred Munnings of 1930 shows the couple mounted on their hunters, one of which, named Portumna after the family's Irish estate, had been given to the princess as a wedding present from 'the Ladies of Ireland'. The last of the great family portraits was done in 1936 by Sir William Nicholson, showing the sixth earl in his robes as a Knight of the Garter. The present Lord Harewood buys pictures now and again – the old library has a fine Winterhalter of the opera diva Adelina Patti, which he bought from the widow of Patti's last husband – but his chief contribution to the contents of Harewood is the bold placing of Epstein's massive marble *Adam*, acquired in 1961, in the Entrance Hall, which has been cleared of its Victorian sofas and antlers and restored to the stark elegance the other Adam first intended. Because of its weight, the Epstein sculpture stands not in the middle but over the junction of walls beneath the hall floor.

Harewood's chief glory, of course, has always been its furniture, a unique series of Chippendale designs specially made for the house and including wonderful *jeux d'esprit* like the carved window pelmets in the Gallery, which deceive even the knowing eye with their cunning folds and draperies. It is here that the true marriage of house and contents occurs, and where the whole is incomparably more than the sum of its parts. Although there was a national furore in 1971 when the Harewood trustees put the Titian up for sale, it had been in the family for only one generation and as a loss to the house (it had anyway been on loan for ten years to the National Gallery) was surely not comparable with the sale six years earlier of the Chippendale library table, one of the greatest marquetry pieces of its time.

In 1947, when the twenty-four-year-old George Lascelles took on his burden of history, no such major sales would have been contemplated; a bit of silver here and there, perhaps, or a few jewels to keep things going. But few of the great English country houses were going to be able to stay the way they had looked and been lived in before 3 September 1939.

9

Struggle for Survival

The new social order which had been so overwhelmingly endorsed at the polls in 1945 came with astonishing speed in the first three years of post-war reconstruction. Blueprints for a socialist Britain, in the shape of white papers and parliamentary bills, poured from the Whitehall presses and were turned into legislation through one weary all-night sitting after another. The mass of civil service and committee work involved was formidable; the national insurance scheme, foundation stone of the welfare state, required two white papers to explain it. In the first year of the Labour government, bills were passed to control investment; to nationalize the mines, Cable and Wireless and the Bank of England; to set up the state-owned airlines, the National Health Service, the new towns and the Atomic Energy Authority. Private enterprise in transport and utilities was rapidly dismantled; the railway companies taken over, the 550 independent electricity companies merged into a central state-controlled authority. The Trades Disputes Act of 1906 was repealed, unfettering the power of organized labour, and farmers were brought into the embrace of the state with a four-year plan for agriculture begun in 1947; its object, triumphantly achieved, was to raise the net output of farming by 20 per cent above that of 1946–47 and 50 per cent over that of 1938.

A new, avowedly redistributive approach to taxation was levelling out the peaks and valleys of pre-war income: by 1951 the standard rate of income tax was 9s. 6d. in the pound, 6d. lower than in the wartime emergency but still nearly double the pre-war level, and other taxes had risen dramatically. Death duties on an estate valued at £100,000, which would have been 20 per cent in 1938, had gone to 50 per cent by 1950; on estates of £1 million, the slice taken by the taxman, 50 per cent in

1938, now amounted to four-fifths. Landowning families increasingly resorted to the device of the estate company, only to find Labour chancellors one jump ahead of them. In 1946 Hugh Dalton changed the tax-exempt period for gifts from three years before death to five years; one unfortunate aristocrat caught by the new law was the tenth Duke of Devonshire, who in 1946 made over 97 per cent of his shares in the Chatsworth company to his family and was just four months inside the tax-exempt period in 1951 when he took an axe to a tree on his estate and died of a heart attack. Continuing the assault on wealth, Sir Stafford Cripps's first budget in 1948 introduced a once-and-for-all capital levy on unearned incomes over £2000 a year. Official statistics charted a measurable shift in the distribution of wealth: in 1938 the 'top 2000' had averaged an income of £43,000 and retained £15,000 of it after tax; in 1956 the same proportion of the British rich averaged £35,000 a year and kept only £6000. At the other end of the scale, Seebohm Rowntree's third survey of the city of York in 1950 showed only 3 per cent of the population below the poverty line, compared with almost one-third in 1936.

This, too, was what the people had voted for in 1945. In the great social changes that were sweeping across the land, few noticed, or cared, that the big landowners were once more being forced to break up their estates. In June 1948 the twenty-first Earl of Shrewsbury and Talbot sold nearly one-third of his lands, some of which had been owned by the family since 1170. In the same month Baron de L'Isle and Dudley sold part of Yorkshire that had been in his family for 400 years. England, it seemed, was changing hands all over again; by 1950 well over a third of all the agricultural holdings in England and Wales were owned by those who farmed them. The struggle against an unsympathetic government and indifferent public opinion prompted some bitter obsequies for the landed classes. Angela Thirkell, herself one of the gentry under siege, doubtless spoke from the heart when she put these words into the mouth of a character in *Love Among the Ruins*, published in 1948: 'We have seen the end of a civilization. It began to crash in 1789 and this is its last gasp. It's a sickening thought, but there it is. All our scrattlings and scutterings, our trying to save a bit here and a bit there, are useless. We are out of date.' Yet the aristocracy, helped perhaps by the fact that there were an increasing number of new landowners in their twenties and thirties, responded in many cases to the rigours of the age with ingenuity, humour and resilience. Lord Shrewsbury, the premier earl of

England, had, it was reported, set up a barrow to sell produce by the road outside the family seat, Ingestre in Staffordshire, and was doing so well that he was thinking of changing it for a caravan. It had to be on wheels, he explained to reporters, to avoid development charges.

The young seventh Earl of Harewood faced a daunting inheritance in 1947. There were the ravages of wartime use and neglect to be made good in the house, the necessity of making do with fewer staff to maintain both house and estate, the position of the widowed Princess Royal to consider and, above all, the newly increased death duties to be paid on the sixth earl's estate. These were levied at £800,000 on an estate of 24,000 acres valued at £1.4 million. In September 1949, the Harewood tenants received a letter from their new landlord saying that he had hoped to preserve the estate in its entirety as his father had left it to him, 'but the burden of death duties is so heavy that I am left with no alternative but to arrange a sale by auction during the summer of 1950. I hope many tenants will find it possible to buy their own holdings. . . .' It was the first substantial sale of Harewood land since the North Riding sale of 1920, and the biggest in the family's history. Altogether, Lord Harewood put one-third of his estates on the market, a total of 7600 acres with a yearly rental value of £10,500. He had already disposed of the Clanricarde estate at Portumna, 1400 acres of County Galway, which had been losing money as farmland since the late 1920s. It was sold to the Irish Land Commission for afforestation.

The auction of the Yorkshire lands took place in June 1950, in the faded 1930s grandeur of the Queen's Hotel, Leeds. The catalogue from Hollis and Webb, the auctioneers, described the sale as being of 'the outlying parts of the Harewood estate' and stated that 'the land for the most part is in good heart'. There were ninety-nine lots and bidding was brisk all day, twenty-seven lots being sold for £58,000 in an hour and a half before the lunch break, twenty-four lots for £94,000 in less than two hours after lunch. Most of the buyers were, as Lord Harewood had hoped, tenants whose families had farmed the land for generations. John J. Dalby, whose forebears had farmed on Harewood lands since the Civil War, paid £12,100 for two farms at East Keswick. Many small deposits, said the *Yorkshire Post*, were paid in cash from rolls of pound notes which 'curled up on the table as if to show how long they had been tied in bundles'. The sale made £256,010 and 90 per cent of the land was bought by its tenant farmers. In the following year more land was sold, including seven villages – Plompton, Spofforth, Weeton, Wigton,

Wike, East Keswick and Kirkby Overblow. In all, 14,600 acres were sold in 1950 and 1951. By the mid-1960s, the estate of 24,000 acres which the sixth earl had bequeathed would be down to 7000 acres.

It was an experience common to the landowners of England in the early 1950s. By 1952, only half the families in *Burke's Landed Gentry* possessed any land at all, compared with two-thirds in 1937. Five hundred peers were listed in *Debrett* as owning country seats, but only 150 still kept them up. Yet, surprisingly, it was a Labour government intent on a social revolution which awoke and responded to the threat facing Britain's unique legacy of country houses. Though no one had kept accurate count, probably as many as 500 had been destroyed between 1890 and 1939. The prospect in 1945 was of yet more piles of rubble as irreplaceable but impossibly costly buildings were sacrificed to the bulldozers. Two imaginative moves by the Attlee government helped to stem the onrush of demolition. One was the Land Fund, the brainchild of the same Chancellor Dalton who had attempted to block the flow of inherited wealth by changing the law on tax-exempt gifts. The other was the appointment by his successor Sir Stafford Cripps in 1948 of a committee under the chairmanship of Sir Ernest Gowers, the distinguished civil servant and author of *Plain Words*, to examine the issues affecting the future of country houses in private hands.

The Land Fund, conceived by Dalton in 1946 as a 'thank-offering for victory', employed money from the sale of war surplus materials to acquire and preserve property of national interest. Although the Inland Revenue had been empowered since 1910 to accept property in lieu of death duties, it had done so only twice in the intervening thirty-six years. The fund would enable the Treasury to compensate the Revenue for taxes lost as a result of such acceptances, and the concept of transfer to the National Trust, feasible since the 1930s but comparatively little used, gained ground rapidly. In 1945 the Trust owned twenty-three country houses; between 1946 and 1950 it acquired nineteen more; between 1951 and 1955 another twelve and between 1956 and 1960 a further twenty-one. Important country houses transferred to the Trust with Land Fund assistance included Shugborough Hall in Staffordshire, seat of the Earls of Lichfield, the splendid Elizabethan Hardwick Hall in Derbyshire and Sissinghurst Castle in Kent. Immediately after the war, there were considerable advantages for owners with large incomes in handing over their houses to the National Trust in return for the right to live in them. As the Gowers Report said: 'A taxpayer who pays 19s. 6d.

in the pound on the top slice of his income may be able, by foregoing only £125 a year of his spendable income, to put £5,000 a year into the hands of the Trust for the upkeep of the house.' This convenient situation did not, however, long survive the onset of inflation. Post-war stringency also came to the rescue of large, unmanageable country houses which were suddenly in demand, due to building controls and the absence of materials, for conversion into schools or local authority offices. But institutional use invariably had a depressing effect and such houses tended to survive only as the shells of their former selves.

The report by Sir Ernest Gowers's committee produced even more lasting effects than those of the Land Fund, leading to the establishment of the Historic Buildings Councils to advise the government on repair grants for buildings of outstanding national importance. At last, and after so much had been lost, public awareness dawned on the need for preservation and conservation. In their first year, 1953, the councils advised the offer of grants totalling £10,656; by 1958 this had risen to £548,597 but in those five years the cost of repairs had risen by 20 per cent. (In 1966 the HBC estimated costs had gone up by 25 per cent in just two years.) Among their many conservation projects, the proportion of HBC grants to country houses is only about one-third, and some of the most historic homes now open to the public, among them Harewood, Chatsworth, Belvoir Castle, Compton Wynyates and Haddon Hall, have been run by their owners without any grants at all.

In 1950, however, such help lay in the future and the way ahead was clouded with uncertainty. As well as selling off a third of his father's lands, Lord Harewood took the decision that year to open part of the house to the public on a regular, paying basis. Since the eighteenth century, in common with aristocratic practice elsewhere, Harewood's state rooms had been open on request on certain days of the year; now, with the opening for economic reasons of Longleat by the Marquess of Bath in 1949, and the removal of petrol rationing early in 1950, the pastime of country house visiting, formerly the preserve of a minority of county gentry, was launched on the mass public as a new form of entertainment. Led by the ebullient Duke of Bedford at Woburn Abbey it was soon to burgeon out into a whole subculture of the leisure industry with safari parks, adventure playgrounds, funfairs, model railways in the grounds and other activities allied more to show business than to the appreciation of architecture, landscape and works of art. By 1954 between 150 and 200 houses were open to the half-crown trippers, and by the end of the fifties it was estimated that between two and three million people were visiting country houses every year.

Lord Harewood was one of the first to perceive that the historic country house would henceforth have to help pay for its own upkeep by becoming a public recreational amenity. For his mother, the Princess Royal, it was inevitably a more difficult adjustment, but one she accepted with fortitude, even though she used to flee to the top woods to watch birds or pick blackberries on the Wednesdays, Thursdays and Saturdays when visitors arrived. The princess, still only in her early fifties, retained Harewood House as her home in a joint arrangement with her son; she may not have relished the idea of strangers tramping through the Adam rooms at 1s. 6d. a head (plus 1s. for the gardens) but she was content with her own wing where she had Edwin Lascelles's State Bedroom as her sitting room, full of books and pictures, the Red Bedroom upstairs over the north front entrance, and rooms for her lady-in-waiting and secretary.

Like everyone else in the country who yearned for pre-war quality again, she met frustration when trying to redecorate her new quarters. Letters survive in the family archives from the London firm of Cowtan and Sons in Grosvenor Gardens, which had done the renovations of 1937 and 1938 to the Breakfast Room and Rose Drawing Room. In response to the princess's request for twenty-five yards of fifty-inch-wide damask for new bedroom curtains, Cowtans found some at £3 5s. a yard which would need no coupons; the cheaper nylon taffeta, 35s. to 40s. a yard, required 2⅔ coupons a yard. Old damask, the firm advised her, was at a premium and could cost as much as £10 a yard. It was hoped, Cowtans wrote, that their weavers, Messrs Warner of Braintree in Essex, would be able to supply her Royal Highness's requirements within a few weeks, 'but they are greatly restricted as to what can be supplied for the Home Market'. In the end she chose a small, all-over woven design in rose and beige at 40s 6d. a yard, which required no coupons.

In London, George VI had given his sister the use of a long, spacious flat under the state rooms of St James's Palace, with an entrance in Engine Court. It had, a former member of the princess's staff remembered, about four public rooms and six bedrooms as well as quarters for the seven permanent servants who maintained it; two would travel with the princess every time she moved between London and Yorkshire. Here, she gave small formal dinner parties and entertained her family:

the king would come for lunch and the 'exiled' Duke of Windsor visited her at least twice a year during his discreet trips to London. Princess Mary had always been close to her eldest brother, even during the trauma of the abdication; one of her rare trips abroad, accompanied by her husband, had been to stay with the ex-king at Enzesfeld Castle near Vienna in 1937. Queen Mary was another regular visitor at Engine Court, always arriving punctually on the last stroke of five and greeting Joe Groom, the old earl's valet who now worked as the princess's London butler, with the same words each time in her curiously deep voice: 'I'm on time again.' In the hall, the royal detective would hand Groom a small wooden box containing precisely two cigarettes, to be placed on the tea table. The old queen and her daughter never lingered over these occasions; an hour was regarded as ample for tea, and when it was over, Queen Mary would leave as briskly as she had come.

As she grew older, the Princess Royal's reserved manner became more intimidating to some, yet what her former staff recall most is the down-to-earth humour, directness and total lack of hauteur of the countrywoman she was at heart. To a workman at Harewood who once called after her retreating back, 'Hey, missis . . .', she replied mildly, 'I'm not your missis' – but went on to ask, courteously, what it was he wanted. On another occasion when Michael Smith, a local caterer, was planning a grand banquet at the house and found that the kitchen had no fresh mint, the princess immediately got into her car and drove to Harrogate to buy some. On a walk in the Mall, a lady-in-waiting was shocked to see her picking up rubbish and carrying it to the nearest litter bin. 'What if someone should see?' she asked nervously. 'I *want* them to see,' replied HRH firmly, 'then perhaps they'll do the same.' Joe Groom still recalls his surprise the first time he saw the Princess setting off for Scotland in the Rolls, seated beside the chauffeur with the lady-in-waiting in the back, luggage cramming the car and overflowing onto the roof, and a packed lunch for eating by the roadside. Spotting birds or deer, she would eagerly hand her binoculars to the nearest servant to share the pleasure.

At Harewood, her life revolved around the gardens, the farm – she was proud of her prize Red Poll herd which was decimated in the foot-and-mouth epidemic of 1960 – and the racing stud on the Otley road which the sixth earl had built up from scratch in 1929, hoping to make it one of the best in the country. The household as she had known it was very different: though in the 1950s there were still eighteen men working in the garden department, as death duties made their impact these were cut to twelve and a strictly commercial approach was adopted. Everything that could be sold must be sold, and new markets found for produce. At one time Harewood was producing 60,000 rose bushes a year, most of which went to a Leeds store. The Princess Royal had been accustomed, pre-war, to having the greenhouses supply enormous quantities of prime quality fruit each year for the table – 600 bunches of grapes, 600 figs (the sixth earl liked them 'rotten ripe', a former gardener remembered), a thousand peaches and nectarines, pears weighing two pounds each, melons and strawberries. In her last years, she became as commercially minded as any and on one occasion instructed the head gardener to change the superb peaches he had sent to the house for some less good: the best, she reminded him, should be sold.

Sunday afternoons were her time for going round the farm and the stud, looking at the animals and chatting to their attendants. Charlie Barnard, the head stud groom, had begun his service with the then Viscount Lascelles at Goldsborough in 1927 as stud hand, earning £1 15s. a week, plus half a crown a night for sitting up with the mares during foaling, three nights a week. After war service as a barrage balloonist he returned to the stud as 'second man' and his pay went up to £1 18s. a week with a night bonus of 5s. In 1954, the princess having decided to carry on the stud after old Lord Harewood's death, he became stud groom at the princely pay of £16 a week – but then received no special night allowance; that was all part of the head man's responsibility. 'I worked seven days a week and enjoyed every minute,' he recalled, ten years after his retirement in 1970. When all the mares had gone away to public stud in the slack time between May and the end of June, he might snatch ten days' holiday. Each August or September the yearlings would go into training at Newmarket. Lord Harewood was 'never a lucky owner', in Barnard's recollection, but the Princess Royal's stud came close to a classic winner with Pretende, sired by the queen's horse Doutelle; Pretende lost the 1966 Derby by a neck to Charlottetown. A more consistently successful horse was Red Dragon, sired by the wartime Derby winner Owen Tudor, which in 1960 won the Vaux Gold Tankard at Redcar, Europe's richest handicap, and earned about £25,000 during its racing career for its South American owner. After a few years running the stud on her own, the Princess Royal leased it to the financier Sir Victor Sassoon, paying 'board' for the mares she continued to stable there.

As the Harewood estate workers returned from war service and the new owner struggled with Treasury demands, there was a gradual resumption of social life, the visitors' book noticeably now reflecting Lord Harewood's interest in the arts and particularly the world of music. One of the earliest visitors, in June 1947, was Anthony Blunt, then a rising art historian fresh from wartime service with MI5 – no one as yet suspecting him of his double life as a Soviet agent. Princess Elizabeth and the Duke of Edinburgh came for three days in July 1949, and the day after they left a young Viennese concert pianist named Marion Stein arrived for a week's stay. On 20 July her engagement to Lord Harewood was announced; the king's consent to the marriage had been obtained and on 29 September she became the new Countess of Harewood. It was, as in the old days, an occasion of almost feudal celebration, with 200 of the West Riding tenants, the farm and estate workers and household staff being taken by special train to London for the grand society wedding in St Mark's, North Audley Street, in the presence of the king and queen, who had travelled south from Balmoral for the ceremony. 'We filled a whole train,' recalled Cliff Lancaster. 'The Princess paid for the train there and back, we just had to pay for our lunch. We got taken to St James's Palace for a buffet do and we were shown into a room with photos of King George. We came back by the 11.30 train from King's Cross. Later in the year there was a big garden party and two men that had been fifty years here were given presents.'

Musical guests now predominated at weekend parties. Peter Pears and Benjamin Britten, who had composed the special wedding anthem, became regular visitors. Artur Rubinstein inscribed his flamboyant signature in the visitors' book in June 1958. There were playwrights, actors and actresses, opera singers, the conductor Carlo Maria Giulini. Concerts were given and grand receptions held for occasions like the annual Leeds Music Festival, of which Lord Harewood became artistic director in 1956. Occasionally, still, the fabulous Lascelles gold and silver plate would be laid out, the head gardener having the task of choosing the best flowers of the season to set it off: crimson chrysanthemums or poinsettias were favoured for their reflections in the gold, and pink carnations or chrysanthemums or a subtle mix of lemon-yellow chrysanthemums and blue flowers – hyacinths or violets – for the silver.

The royal connection was regularly maintained: the new queen, Lord

Harewood's first cousin and niece of the Princess Royal, came on several visits during the 1950s, as did Prince Philip and Princess Margaret. Whenever royalty came to stay it was still the custom for them to plant a tree in the park and for the village to be given a half-day off work. The two generations in the house, the Princess Royal and the earl and countess, coexisted comfortably in their separate sections – Lord and Lady Harewood using the east wing which had traditionally been the main family quarters since Edwin Lascelles's day. In due course a bedroom and dressing room over the Library were converted into day and night nurseries for the three sons of the marriage. When both the princess and the young family were in residence, they dined together in the Spanish Library, the former Breakfast Room renamed from its Spanish leather hangings which the sixth earl had acquired in the late 1930s from the Rothschild mansion at 148 Piccadilly. The Library itself became a communal drawing room.

The first paying visitors in 1950 were permitted to see just five of the state apartments. They came through the pillared Entrance Hall, glimpsed the grand staircase (nowadays enclosed within the private apartments) and circulated round the Rose Drawing Room, the Green Drawing Room, the Gallery, the Dining Room and the Music Room. Even with this restricted access, Harewood became an immediate tourist attraction, and in the late 1950s the Harewoods moved upstairs to a new suite of apartments carved out of bedrooms on the first floor overlooking the north front. This released most of the east wing to public view and in 1958 the designer and artistic adviser Richard Buckle restored the small room known as the Little Library, where the Princess Royal had kept books and ornaments, to its original Adam decoration, reconstructing the alcoves as settings for the magnificent Sèvres porcelain collected by Beau Lascelles during the Regency.

Virtually all the ground floor was now open to the public with the exception of the Princess Royal's sitting room, Lord Harewood's personal sitting room and – on occasions when the family was using it – the Library. In 1959, to mark the bi-centenary of the house, Buckle established a permanent exhibition on its history in the Carr stable block; a new cafeteria was opened, also in the stable block, and a car park and lavatories installed for the visitors. The huge appeal of historic houses to the public had exceeded all expectations, and all over the country owners who had opened their homes on a more or less amateur basis were finding themselves running whole new businesses, requiring investment, additional staff and professional management skills. It was, in many ways, the saving of England's country houses. At the same time, agricultural land was shooting up in value along with other forms of real estate, making many landowners millionaires on paper although that did not necessarily help with the repair costs.

Evelyn Waugh came to regard much of his novel *Brideshead Revisited*, first published in 1945 when prospects looked grim for the owners of great houses, as 'a panegyric preached over an empty coffin'. In a new preface in 1959 he wrote: 'It was impossible to forecast, in the spring of 1944, the present cult of the English country house. It seemed then that the ancestral seats which were our chief artistic achievement were doomed to decay and spoliation like the monasteries in the sixteenth century. . . . Brideshead today would be open to trippers, its treasures rearranged by expert hands and the fabric better maintained than it was by Lord Marchmain. And the English aristocracy has maintained its identity to a degree that then seemed impossible.'

But visitors at 1s 6d. a head, and even the sale of a third of the Harewood acres, could not raise enough money to keep the Treasury and the repair bills at bay. In June 1951 came the first of the big postwar sales of Harewood treasures, including much crested family silver and a black and gold lacquered commode attributed to Chippendale. It was sold by the Princess Royal for £483; in 1973 it was again put on the market by the executors of Sir James Horlick, of the malted milk fortune, and realized 31,000 guineas. More furniture was sold in 1957 along with old masters, rolls of Chinese wallpaper made specially for the house, and a fifty-seven piece Minton dinner service.

The 1960s brought further financial burdens. Labour governments increased the squeeze on landowners by introducing capital gains tax, though not as severely as initially framed, when it would have become payable on the contents of houses when they were inherited as well as sold, thus breaking up many fine collections. This was averted by the energetic lobbying of the Historic Buildings Councils, as was a 1962 proposal to abolish tax relief on repairs, which would have forced owners to pay out of already taxed income.

The first half of the sixties also brought natural disaster and family grief to Harewood. The great gale of March 1962, compounding the damage wrought by an earlier one in March 1956, destroyed not only twenty thousand fine old trees on the estate, but also part of one of the two remaining towers on the medieval castle. 'Two centuries of timber growth', the head gardener recalled, went in two nights of fearsome wind. Two-hundred-year-old oaks were plucked out of the ground; cedars of Lebanon and stately old beeches 'sprawled on top of each other'. The gale also badly damaged the roof of Harewood House and was a prime cause of the biggest of the Harewood sales of the sixties. Then, one Sunday afternoon in March 1965, while strolling with her son and grandchildren by the lake, the sixty-seven-year-old Princess Royal collapsed and died. Virtually the whole of the royal family came to the funeral at Harewood parish church, which was conducted by the Archbishop of York: the queen, Prince Philip, Prince Charles, the Queen Mother, Princess Margaret and Princess Marina. The Duke of Windsor had just undergone an eye operation and was advised not to travel to Yorkshire; instead, he and the Duchess attended the memorial service in Westminster Abbey. At Harewood, it was very definitely the end of an era. The princess's sitting room and her other apartments on the ground floor were added to those open to the public and more family heirlooms, including her jewellery and orders of chivalry, put up for sale at Christie's.

In 1963 Lord Harewood had sold the Clanricarde collection of gold snuffboxes for £32,000, but in the year of the Princess Royal's death, treasures from Harewood fetched over half a million pounds in a series of sales at Christie's between May and July 1965. The prize piece was Chippendale's superb library table made to the design of Robert Adam, a neoclassical masterpiece, which fetched £43,000, at that time a record for a single piece of English furniture. It was later acquired by Leeds Corporation and placed on permanent display in Temple Newsam, the great Elizabethan-Jacobean mansion overlooking the Aire valley which is run by the city as a museum. In June 1965 came the big sale which was to pay, among other things, for the gale damage three years earlier. It included eleven paintings by Gainsborough, Girtin, Sandby and others; sixty-six superb Sèvres vases collected by Beau Lascelles; eighty old masters collected by the sixth earl, and a magnificent group of Regency silver-gilt which had been shown at the Regency Exhibition in the Royal Pavilion, Brighton, in 1951 as part of the Festival of Britain. These pieces, by the master silversmith Paul Storr, had been made for Edward Lascelles, the first earl, between 1814 and 1816, and comprised dessert stands, candelabra and wine-coolers. Other silver treasures of the Harewood strongrooms which went to Christie's that June represented three generations of Lascelles and their families by marriage, as revealed by the engraved arms. There was also a group of Charles I and Charles II wine cups and vases acquired by the sixth earl after the First World War from the thirteenth Earl of Home, father of the present Lord Home. The silver made £131,810, at the time a record figure for a personal collection. A week earlier, the famous Harewood Gold Vase, a first-century Roman piece which had held a proud place in the house in a setting specially designed by Richard Buckle, was sold for £11,550.

The sale of the Princess Royal's jewels in October 1970, including her favourite sunburst tiara and diamond star badge as Dame Commander of the Order of the British Empire, was the first important sale of jewels belonging to royalty since that of the Russian crown jewels in the 1920s. The thirty pieces realized £78,000, the tiara alone going for £7000. The princess herself had already sold five splendid pieces in November 1960 for £81,200; an earlier sale after her death had made £52,800.

But the biggest and most controversial sale was to come in June 1971. This was of the Titian painting, *The Death of Actaeon*, another of the sixth earl's acquisitions. It had formerly hung in the Green Drawing Room at Harewood House but since 1961 had been on loan to the National Gallery. Christie's guarded the news of the impending sale by the Harewood trustees with scrupulous care, but it reckoned without a sharp-eyed lady from Devon who had happened to read in *The Times* some weeks earlier about the existence of a list of major paintings in private hands which museums and galleries would be keen to acquire if ever they came on the market. One of these paintings was the Harewood Titian at the National Gallery. The Devonshire lady subsequently visited the National Gallery and looked for the Titian. It was nowhere to be seen. She asked the attendants; no one could enlighten her, except to suggest that perhaps it was being cleaned. Not satisfied, she returned home and wrote a letter to *The Times* about the missing Titian; the letters editor smelled a story and a reporter was assigned to making inquiries of the two major auction houses, Christie's and Sotheby's. At that precise moment, Christie's public relations office was preparing a press release on the sale, under strict embargo. A round of frantic telephoning to Fleet Street news editors was needed to ensure that an announcement of such magnitude to the art world broke in orderly fashion.

The sale itself lasted just eighty-five seconds before the Titian was knocked down to an American art dealer named Julius Weitzner for £1,680,000. When it emerged that his purchase was destined to leave the country for the Getty Museum in Malibu, California, there was a storm of protest. It was a sensitive time for the sale of great works of art from British ownership and a swelling stream of treasures had been allowed to go abroad, culminating in the sale of a Velasquez portrait from the Earl of Radnor's collection for £2 million to the Californian industrialist Norton Simon. Eventually the Heath government agreed to make money available to match the Titian's sale figure and the picture returned to its niche in the National Gallery.

Sales of furniture continued in the 1970s; in April 1976 thirty pieces of Chippendale went for £39,000, including a rare marquetry-top table and fourteen dining chairs made for Goldsborough Hall. Small parcels of land and buildings were also sold off: in 1974 a set of buildings known as Hollin Hall Cottages, which had been used as the setting for the Yorkshire Television series 'Follifoot Farm', were put up for sale by the Harewood estate but failed to find a buyer; they were later sold privately to a Leeds solicitor for £10,000. Harewood village was showing signs of change: in 1960 the historic old toll bar house at Harewood Bridge which had been the scene of the 1753 turnpike riot was pulled down by Wetherby Rural District Council as unsafe. A dozen council houses went up in the late 1950s, but architecturally rather special ones; built of local stone from demolished old cottages, they toned in with Carr's eighteenth-century terraces.

As well as the dispersal of art treasures in the saleroom, the late 1960s saw the break-up of the Harewood marriage; inevitably, because of his close relationship with the queen, conducted in the glare of press publicity. The divorce in 1967 was followed by Lord Harewood's marriage to another talented musician, the Australian Patricia Tuckwell, sister of Barry Tuckwell, the internationally renowned horn player. A few years later Marion, Countess of Harewood, married the Liberal politician Jeremy Thorpe, to whom she had been introduced by their mutual friend, the concert pianist Moura Lympany. The new Lady Harewood immediately took a practical and active interest in the running of the house and its business side; together she and Lord Harewood decided that, although an extra attraction in the grounds was clearly needed, they did not want to follow in the steps of those historic house owners who had installed safari parks and funfairs. The Bird Garden, opened in 1970, was the successful compromise. It was a novelty among the stately homes; the concept sensitively fitted the contours of the park; the exotic birds adapted well to their unlikely home in

Capability Brown's landscape, and it was an immediate crowd puller. Between 1967 and 1972 the annual count of visitors to the house rose spectacularly from 64,000 to 263,000.

In twenty years, the role of Harewood House had changed irrevocably. Now a family house only at Easter and Christmas and for a few weeks in winter when the state rooms were relieved of their velvet ropes and given back to daily living, with the owners themselves little more than weekend visitors, the pride of Adam, Carr and Chippendale was fulfilling its late twentieth-century destiny as part of the 'leisure industry'. In the view of some, this was the sort of asset which a post-industrial Britain would increasingly come to represent to the world.

10

Harewood at Work: Making History Earn its Keep

An early morning towards the end of May. Harewood House still sleeps on its gritstone escarpment, tall windows turned blindly to the splendid view beyond Sir Charles Barry's south-facing terrace. The rising sun strikes over the shoulder of the house, bringing its yellow-buff stone to life and silvering the dull pewter of Capability Brown's lake, wrinkled by a light breeze. This is quintessential England, as the nobleman in these parts has seen it for three hundred years. In the foreground, black St Kilda sheep graze beneath banks of early flowering purple heather falling away under the terrace balustrade. Beyond the lake, fresh green fields, woods folded into their seams, rise gently to the horizon, where gaps in Brown's majestic woodscape still bear witness to the devastating storm of March 1962. In one of the gaps, at a position approximately two o'clock to a watcher on the terrace, an alien shape can be dimly discerned – the twentieth century intruding on the eighteenth. It is the top of a high-rise office building in Leeds, whose industrial grime, noise and concrete are only eight miles away.

The illusion of unchanging tranquillity and leisured ease, enchanting as it is, in fact is only that – an illusion. Although the seventh Earl of Harewood, the eighth of the Lascelles family to own this house and lands, will soon arrive off the London train for the weekend, the day will bring him a very different set of problems and concerns from those which preoccupied his feudal forebears. For Harewood House, like most of England's premier historic homes, is now a highly geared business enterprise, an important flywheel in the leisure industry. Even now, as Geoff Hall, head gardener for twenty-six years in succession to his father, strolls down from his house to be at the greenhouses by 7.30 – he likes to water the tomatoes before the sun gets at them – the first coach-load of school-children, ninety-five of them today, will be setting out in order to arrive at the arched stone entrance to the park soon after ten. School parties form a sizeable slice of the paying visitors to Harewood – an average of 48,000 a year, accompanied by 5500 teachers – and a day in peak season can see as many as 1700, when the time allotted for each party to spend in the house, Bird Garden, Butterfly House and shops has to be planned with the stopwatch timing of a military operation.

Geoff Hall is one of the earliest on the job at Harewood, but Colin and Hilda Stanley, the resident caretakers who live in a basement flat underneath Harewood House, are also busy by 7.30. The Stanleys and some domestic staff are year-round occupants of Harewood, although David Lloyd Jones, music director of Opera North (of which Lord Harewood is vice-chairman), and his wife Carol have a top-floor suite loaned to them while they are in the North. The Stanleys and their part-time helpers from the village have the public rooms of the house cleaned and ready for the new day's crowds by 10.30, in time for the house-opening at eleven. There are seventeen rooms open to the public, not all of vast proportions, arranged in a convenient quadrangle around the outer rim of the ground floor and capable of being toured with reasonable thoroughness in forty minutes. But even so, in a year the cleaners will walk thirty-three miles just vacuuming the main carpet.

The Stanleys are perfectionists, held in considerable awe by their village helpers, and the cleaning is done on a precise system laid down by Colin Stanley, with basic work such as carpets and druggets done daily and two of the seventeen rooms finished thoroughly each day with ornaments dusted and furniture polished, so that the whole house is covered in the course of just over a week. Some of the carpets are as frail and delicate as wall tapestries, especially the one in the Rose Drawing Room, and the vacuum cleaners, built for more robust work, can lift them off the floor, so the helpers take care to avoid the more threadbare areas.

Eight a.m., and the rest of the garden staff, five in all, arrive and are given their instructions for the day: Geoff Hall sends two of them to replant the terrace beds with violas instead of stocks and dispatches two more to mow the grass. In the old days, when Hall joined as a fifteen-year-old apprentice, there were twenty-two gardeners at Harewood, each man with his speciality: a vine man, a carnation man and so on. The agent, Neville Ussher, who joined in 1953, the same year Hall took over, recalls that every time an aeroplane went over and the men stopped to watch, it was reckoned to cost the estate half a crown. In the early fifties fresh fruit, flowers and vegetables were sent daily to the earl's London home during the season. Hall still sends produce down by British Rail's Red Star express parcels service, but not as frequent nor as exotic a selection – in 1979 the Harewoods' Maida Vale house was supplied at intervals with broad beans ('they're still too big,' complained Lord Harewood to Hall, 'they should be no bigger than my little fingernail'), bobby beans, seakale, asparagus, artichokes and tomatoes, with a selection of fruit – strawberries to the fore – but far less hothouse produce, a concession to increased fuel costs. Hall has also stopped the supply of year-round pot plants for sale in the shops; and the walled garden which once grew acres of peas, beans and strawberries for the Lascelles household will now be turned over to sheep. Years ago, Geoff Hall was asked by the Princess Royal, the present earl's mother, 'If this was your own place, what would you do with it?' 'Well, Your Royal Highness,' he replied, 'I'd keep chickens in the greenhouses and I'd plant the rest to forest trees.' The princess, Hall recalls now with a chuckle, was stumped for a reply, but times have caught up at least in part with his ideas for more productive use of the land.

The soil at Harewood, a thin covering over the local millstone grit, is a light loam inclined to acid and ideal for rhododendrons, the abiding glory of the gardens. Geoff Hall, a tall, well-built man with blunt good looks and cropped grey hair who seems younger than his sixty-five years, has made it a point of pride to keep rhododendrons in flower eight months of the year; most people, he says, don't realize there are that many seasonal varieties of the plant. Hall's empire covers twenty-seven acres and 16,000 square feet of glasshouses. Working under him in 1979 were Alan Mason, thirty, the former head gardener at nearby Bramham Park, stately home of the Lane-Fox family, who was due to succeed Hall on his retirement that autumn; a former German prisoner-of-war named Otto Geller; Patrick Bailey, thirty-seven; John Bates, thirty-two, and Julie Stanbridge, twenty, who helped in the greenhouses. The building of the adventure playground in 1969–70 on the hill behind the house 'took eighty per cent of the vandalism out of my department,' says Hall. He and his men used to have to go round every day picking wastepaper bins out of the lake and retrieving notices which had been uprooted and flung into the bushes.

On this particular Friday in late May, Hall has called in two pensioners from Harewood village to assist with the spraying of young conifer plants, holding the infant trees apart with boards while the gardeners spray them with pesticide. Meanwhile in the forestry department, nine strong under head forester Bert Meredith, one woodman has been dispatched to mend an estate road with hot tarmac, all part of the continual cost-cutting that agent Ussher must juggle and improvise each day. ('I know perfectly well if I'd had a contractor in to do the potholes, that would have taken two or three men two days and the bill would have been something under £2000. I said this is nonsense, send the woods tractor five miles to get a load of hot tarmac, we'll hire a roller and the woodman will do the roads. The stuff will cost perhaps £400 and the roller £100, but we're paying the woodman's wages anyway, whether he's looking after trees Lord Harewood couldn't fell until he's a hundred and fifty or mending the roads. So that little job gets done for £500 instead of £1500.')

By 8.45, David Wrench, the house opening manager, is leaping out of his tomato-red estate car at the unpretentious Georgian house which was once Harewood's vicarage and now serves as the estate offices. Wrench is rangy, eager, with a thatch of prematurely grey hair over a ruddy country complexion, invariably sucking on a sweet-smelling pipe. He came to Harewood in 1968 'out of mail order and law', as he puts it, having spent five years in his father's law practice and five years with Grattan's Warehouses. In his career at Harewood he has, at one time or another, done everything himself from whipping up bacon and eggs under the grill in the cafeteria to cleaning the lavatories and directing the cars.

'I was very lucky to come here when tourism was taking off in the late sixties. The year I came we had 61,000 visitors – by 1970, with the opening of the Bird Garden, it was up to 246,000. Since then the lowest it's been was 260,000 and the highest 300,009. They all swear that I went out into the road and stopped cars just to get that last nine! We can get a good return from 275,000, and that's really as much as the estate can comfortably stand in the peak months – late May, June, July, and August. But there is room for growth at other times, that's why we've started opening in the winter months; there are always people on holiday, and there will be more with time to spare as the retirement age is brought down. On a winter's day we can get anything from one to 1500 visitors, but we're quite happy with 50 a day. We work on a fixed staff at that time of year and they would be there anyway. It would be a misnomer to call it a profit, but it's certainly a hefty contribution to the running costs.'

Harewood House, unlike its farm, is not run as a limited company, but it is administered on similar business lines if you imagine Lord Harewood as chairman, Neville Ussher as managing director and the heads of department as divisional directors, each with his budgetary limits and forecasts, for the house, the Bird Garden, forestry and gardens. Each detail is costed precisely and weighed against target: the 'project books' on Harewood compiled by a professional teacher and given free to schoolchildren, for instance, cost the estate 8p apiece. Although that is a loss on the admission charge for each child, it is calculated that he or she will spend on average another 75p on gifts, ice-cream, snacks and souvenirs, so the outlay is reckoned worthwhile as well as providing a genuine educational tool. (There is a study centre with permanent exhibition in the elegant stable block designed by Harewood's first architect, John Carr, which school parties are encouraged to use.)

At the peak of the season, the house provides employment for forty-five, including the catering department which, when turnover reached £50,000, was handed over to a professional hotel catering company from Leeds. The ages of the house staff range from twenty-two to sixty-four. The basic year-round workforce is only twenty-two, eight of them women, supplemented by part-timers from the village who come in as needed for two or three days a week. The Harewood payroll for the whole estate is incredibly modest by the standards of half a century ago – eighty-five with odd helpers bringing it up to a maximum ninety-two.

Wrench's wife Judith works with him, her first task each morning being to count the cash takings which have been brought up the previous evening by Tom McGrath, a retired policeman who acts as Wrench's eyes and ears on the estate. McGrath arrives at ten each morning and does not leave until the last visitor is safely off the grounds. The cash passed over daily to Securicor can range, according to the time of year and weather, from £300 up to 'a frightening amount of money' which, for understandable reasons, Wrench is reluctant to spell out. From Judith's figures he makes up the profit and loss sheet for each 'cash day', from which he will compile a weekly report for Lord Harewood and Neville Ussher. The admission pricing structure is complex enough on its own – twenty-nine different classifications, including tickets for the house only, the park or Bird Garden only, group discounts and so on (one teacher comes free with every ten children). In early 1979 the all-in ticket covering the house and all its ancillary attractions was still only £1 before reductions for groups and pensioners, but inflation and soaring fuel costs were pushing it inexorably to a 50 per cent increase by 1980. By 1982 it had risen to £2.

Wrench likes to get in early while it is still quiet ('two or three hours here on a Sunday morning is fabulous; I can do more then than in three normal working days') before pelting off in his car to visit admission control ('very important, like reception in a hotel; that's where the customer is met, so the attendants must to a certain extent also be PROs and salesmen'), check on coach arrivals and dash in for a brief exchange with the motherly ladies who man the house admission desk, the shops and the cafeteria in Carr's stately stable block.

In the course of his rounds he picks up a fund of stories; the raw material of the historic homes business is people, and no two days are ever routinely alike. There was the time when a man dressed in full cowboy rig rode up to the north portico, dismounted with a flourish and demanded that someone look after his horse while he toured the house, and the time an old lady got shut into the Bird Garden, which closes at 6.15, and was discovered next morning sleeping peacefully under a briar bush. Her family, incredibly, had not only failed to notice that Granny was missing on their return home, but were irate to be summoned back to Harewood next day to fetch her. And there was the occasion of a traction engine rally when a woman driving to Sheffield automatically followed the hand signals of a policeman, only to find herself immovably locked into the stream of cars heading for the rally. She had wondered, she said mildly, why there should be a diversion through a field.

The great British public at play, Wrench finds to his amusement, is extraordinarily regimented in its habits. After he put up a notice saying 'Please Park Anywhere On the Grass', and visitors persisted in parking side by side in neat rows, he decided to conduct a test. 'I drove in one day and put my car bang in the middle of six acres of grass, and waited for the first car to come in. And do you know, he parked so close to mine that I had to get out on the passenger's side. The same thing happened with the next car, and the next. So I asked one or two people why, when the notice clearly said park anywhere you like, they had chosen to park in a line, and some got quite offensive: "Mind your own bloody business, I'll park where I like," they said. Incredible.'

Wrench has one reason to be grateful for such conformity, however: Harewood has suffered no serious vandalism or theft since its opening.

Like every other public institution it must take account of
security against the political saboteur, and is equipped with a
battery of sophisticated and subtle devices for that purpose – just as
well, considering the sublime innocence of some of its part-time guar-
dians. At the height of the IRA bombing campaign in Britain, to test the
alertness of his staff, Wrench made up a 'bomb' out of a cigarette
packet, torch batteries and wires. He left it half-hidden by a radiator, just
visible enough to anyone making a routine check. After three days had
passed without it being discovered, he went to a telephone booth in the
village, put a handkerchief over his mouth and phoned the house. One
of the pensioner stewards answered. Wrench said through his handkerchief: 'There's a bomb in Harewood House.' 'Yer what?' came the
uncomprehending Yorkshire voice. 'There's a bomb in Harewood
House,' he repeated impatiently, and put the phone down. A few hours
later he called in at the house. The same old man was at the desk. Had
anything unusual happened? 'No-ooo,' came the slow reply. Nothing
out of the ordinary at all, no phone calls for instance? 'Oh, there was a
silly old man on the telephone who said there was a bomb in the house, I
think, but he didn't leave his name.' Today, even the oldest of
Harewood's custodians are implanted with the need for vigilance,
though not long after the 'bomb' episode, a man asked one of the
women attendants to look after his carrier bag while he went round the
house. When Wrench discovered what had happened, he had the bag
isolated, summoned the police and, very cautiously, they tested its contents. The bewildered owner, meanwhile, had been rounded up and
ironically proved to have a criminal record: he had, in fact, just been
released from prison that morning, and all his worldly possessions were
in that carrier bag.

The Wrenches live only a mile and half from the estate, so the six-day
week he works at the height of the season is not oppressive when he can
slip back for a couple of hours' gardening in between a morning in York
chairing a meeting of the Yorkshire Tourist Board on marketing and
publicity, going on local radio to recruit a part-time litter-picker, and
deciding whether to hire out two fields to caravans at £1000 a field,
balancing the cash flow (and potential spending power of the caravan-
ners) against the loss to farming use.

Still, as a working life it operates on distinctly 'unsocial hours', as the
industrial jargon has it. As Wrench says, 'In this business you are putting twelve months' work into six: even if you're open all year the bulk

of the work is crammed into those six.' Harewood in fact is open now for ten months of the year: in December and January the house reverts to family use, with the beautiful Adam library becoming once again a place for reading and conversation. Winter is the time to catch up on essential maintenance and restoration, though costs here are shooting up so alarmingly that it will be a long time before another room is as lavishly restored as the Entrance Hall in 1967–68 at a cost then of £4500. In 1972–73 three centuries of Leeds grime was sandblasted off the fine old gritstone of the exterior at a cost of £20,000: today, Wrench reckons, you could multiply that four or five times.

Paraphrasing Harold Wilson's aphorism about a week in politics, Wrench likes to say that seven days is a long time in the historic house business. 'You just never know how it's going to go: on the Spring Bank Holiday weekend in 1977 we had 8400 over the four days; the year before it was 23,000, though admittedly then we had a veteran car rally as well. In 1973 it was 18,000. All you can do is gear your staff for what you think is going to keep them nicely busy, and get in part-time help accordingly.'

On this particular day, the weather has turned chill and cloudy after early sun. There is a hint of rain, but this early in the season it's not likely to be busy anyway. At 11 a.m. sharp the first visitors are in the marble-floored entrance hall with its mock porphyry columns of dark red, a group of Yorkshire women in sensible cardigans and light coats. A few pay 50p extra to hire a portable tape recorder with Lord Harewood's personal commentary ('Welcome to my home') telling them of his favourite bits of Sèvres and offering the aside that his mother, the Princess Royal, always hated the portrait of her drawn by John Singer Sargent because 'she had hay-fever at the time and she thought it showed.'

In the first of the two China Rooms, filled with the famous Sèvres collection and a gold and white Crown Derby dinner service which once belonged to the statesman George Canning, Herbert Green the house carpenter comes through to turn on the lights. Small, bespectacled, bald, like a benevolent gnome in his brown linen coat with a wooden rule sticking out of the top pocket, Herbert is sixty-four and the oldest of the full-time workers. He has served the estate for forty-nine years and is due for retirement in a few months. He came as a wheelwright and joiner when 'it was all carts and wagons', but after the war, he became a general carpenter, making window frames, doors and staircases. Just before the Princess Royal died in 1965 he was promoted to house carpenter. 'They were strict in those days. You weren't allowed to go where you liked, you had to find out where the Princess was first. We were supplied with slippers and house gloves – we weren't allowed to touch the furniture with our bare hands.' When the house was first opened to the public 'it was a bit strange like, after everything being set out for the Lord and Lady. Things have gone for the worse in my opinion. I'd rather have it as it was – you knew what you were doing.' The room we were in, restored by Richard Buckle in 1958 to its original Adam design, adjoins what is still called the Princess Royal's dressing room, and Herbert Green remembers it as her 'parcels room' – piled so high with parcels of books, stationery and presents brought up from London that 'it was a job to get in that door'.

The visitors file through respectfully. A studious-looking American woman, her white-haired husband faintly comic in a bobbled beret, peers intently at the beautiful joinery of a heavy mahogany door. As Neville Ussher says, people are often more fascinated by the small, mundane details of the historic house – the door handles, window catches, hair brushes, 'the kind of mat they wipe their feet on' – than in the museum-piece furniture. These are things they can relate to objects bought for their own homes, bought perhaps in a chain store; the difference in quality in such details impresses more than a Chippendale bureau-bookcase.

In Lord Harewood's Sitting Room, a cheerful, chintz-furnished room facing south to the lake and east over the gardens, old Charlie Greaves, lamed by a footballing injury in his salad days, sits stiffly on a chair which enables him to command a view through three rooms in a row. He is seventy-seven and has 'been with the family', as he puts it, for fifty-four years, forty-two of them as a forester. Now he is a part-time house steward, like several other estate pensioners, and thinks he holds the record for length of service at Harewood, challenged only by Teddy Salmon, the retired chauffeur – 'there's mebbe a month between us.' Salmon is eighty-four and also works as a steward. Greaves, like most of the pensioners, remembers the old days with affection. 'Life was what you made it, it was quite a nice life. Wages were small but we seemed to have a good time.' He used to work in the house nearly every Christmas, helping with the piles of luggage as the family converged and humping in the 'faggots and chips' for kindling the fires. When the coal grew low in the arched underground coal houses, now grassed over, two hundred tons would be brought up from the mines at Garforth by local farmers who earned 2s. a load for carrying it up by horse and cart.

Greaves's memory not only spans the sixth earl's time but goes back to the present earl's grandfather, the fifth earl, a country landowner in the old style with a passion for shooting, fishing and rearing pheasants. (Curiously, though, he didn't plant a single tree in his period, a serious omission eighty years on, when the timber would have been coming to maturity.) There were ten or twelve foresters when Greaves came in 1925 – 'there was nothing commercial then, it was just keeping the estate nice and tidy'. At the peak of Harewood's timber production the woods staff numbered around thirty; it has now reverted to ten. The big gale of March 1962 is still fresh in his memory. 'We were out thirty-six hours in it – you couldn't get off the estate, north, south, east or west, because all the roads were blocked. Everything just tipped up, tree on top of tree. I've never seen anything like it. Twenty thousand big ones came down, we had some beautiful oaks, all lifted up by the roots – two hundred, three hundred cubic feet, some of 'em were.' As the wind scythed its track of destruction across the woods, the trees 'pushed each other down like skittles'. It took two years to clear the debris.

Noon, and the visitors are beginning to bunch up in the Princess Royal's Sitting Room, hung with landscapes of Wharfedale. Some, listening to Lord Harewood's taped voice through their head-sets, conscientiously turn from side to side comparing the two celebrated views of the house from the south-east: Girtin's 'rather apocalyptic' treatment with storm clouds sweeping up from the west, Turner's bathed peacefully in autumn sunlight. The schoolchildren, aged ten or so, scribble obediently in their project books and shuffle into the Spanish Library with its shelves of books on architecture, Chippendale, Sargent, *De Groot's Catalogue of XVII Century Dutch Painters*, and then, unexpectedly, a whole wall of bound volumes of *Punch*, like any middlebrow country house. On the left, by the entrance to the Rose Drawing Room, there is a painting of Christ at the column by a fifteenth-century Florentine artist, showing Jesus stripped to the waist. A Scottish matron, not realizing the religious nature of the picture, exclaims skittishly to her friend, 'Oh, we're getting into the interesting stuff now.'

By 12.20 the sun is fitfully breaking through again, and there are twenty cars and five coaches in the car park; busier than an average Friday so far. At some stage, unobserved by the public, Lord and Lady Harewood have slipped in through their own front door, crossed the hall diagonally and disappeared through a door on the right leading to the main staircase, which visitors never see. This weekend, in their eight-roomed flat arranged round a square lobby on the first floor, they have a writer from the *New Yorker* staying with them, absorbing with the photographic detail of that magazine's leisurely essays two days in the life of this highly uncharacteristic member of the British aristocracy and royal family. Tonight the party will drive to Newcastle for a performance by the Scottish National Opera, tomorrow morning to Leeds for a recital at Leeds Grammar School and in the evening, after opening a Rover car rally in the grounds, back to Leeds town hall for a concert. On Sunday Sir Clifford Curzon, the pianist, arrives for a short stay and there's another recital to be attended at Leeds town hall. Monday offers a breathing space and a chance to scan the financial reports on house and farm, and first thing on Tuesday it is back to London and Lord Harewood's office at the Coliseum. A typical weekend that will be repeated, with variations of musical events and house guests, perhaps forty times in the year.

Lord Harewood might or might not have time this weekend to see Neville Ussher, who has a few things he wants to discuss. Ussher has just driven back from a morning spent in Leeds with the farm consultants, who periodically run a slide rule over the management strategy of the farming company, and with the Rivers Board to discuss a flooding problem in the forty-seven-acre site the family owns in the centre of York. He is an impressive, tweedy man in his middle fifties who could easily be taken for the owner of Harewood. He has a big presence and a staccato way of addressing a stranger until he relaxes, when he can break into an infectious giggle at something he has just said. His office is the nerve centre of Harewood with its large leather-topped table littered with ordnance maps and plans and sheets of accounts. A large-scale map pinned to one wall shows how the Harewood territory has shrunk: 'Twenty years ago you could ride from here to Goldsborough and never be off Harewood land, and Goldsborough estate alone, as you can see from the pink area, was bigger than Harrogate.' But the estates, already reduced from 23,000 acres after the war to 7000-odd when Ussher came in 1953, have since been almost exactly halved – 3316.098, as another wallchart details with precision. Including some land administered as a trust, the estate Ussher now looks after amounts in all to 4821.589 acres. This embraces the 1650-acre home farm, run as a separate trading company. Ussher personally put that together, gathering in tenanted farms as their occupants died off or left, and adding them to the original nucleus of 320 acres. The result, with a dairy herd of 500 cows producing nearly £500,000 worth of milk a year, pigs, sheep and some beef cattle, is an intensively farmed and healthily profitable business.

An agent handling an estate like this – in Scotland he would be called a factor – must combine in one person a variety of professional skills, any one of which would furnish a full-time career: managing director chartered surveyor, farmer, accountant, lawyer, forester and valuer. Ussher, like Lord Harewood – they are of an age – spent most of the war in a German prison camp. Afterwards, both were appointed ADCs to the Governor General of Canada, the Earl of Athlone, and Ussher first met Viscount Lascelles, as he then was, on London's Waterloo Station en route to board the *Queen Elizabeth* for the Atlantic crossing. After Canada, Ussher spent some time in the Ministry of Agriculture, managed an uncle's estate as a land agent and farmed for three years on his own account, 'milking my own cows, which I loved', before the call came from Lord Harewood. He said his old agent, who had been there for thirty-five years, was dying – would Ussher come up and run things, starting on Monday? 'The Princess Royal thought I was much too young at thirty-three to be let loose on the whole estate,' he chuckles. 'Lord Harewood just said, well, there's the office and here are the keys, over to you.'

Ussher arrived after the traumatic inheritance period, when the young earl, twenty-four years old and only just out of the army, was pitchforked into the problems of administering an aristocratic estate in austere, Socialist, post-war Britain, with more than £2 million to find in death duties – a full 70 per cent on everything his father had owned. The big land sales of 1950 and 1951 have been followed in Ussher's time by the sale of bits of woodland that had ceased to produce income and, more recently, by that of the Harewood Arms, an old coaching inn with a dozen bedrooms now owned by a local brewery chain, and the neat Georgian estate cottages as they become released from their tied tenancies. Some rents are still as low as £1 a week although others have gone to a more realistic level of £7 a week. At current market prices, they easily fetch £15,000 or more.

The new earl soon decided it was time to take a twentieth-century approach to maintaining a huge historic country house, and he opened it to the public on a limited scale until the Princess Royal died in 1965, when it became possible to open up what had been her private apartments. In the early 1970s, another 1200 acres were sold off to boost the investment portfolio which provides the family's living expenses and which had been depleted to 'almost nought' after payment of the estate duties. In addition, five farms were hived off in a 1959 settlement to provide for the future of Harewood and the junior members of the family.

'So that's about what we've got left,' says Ussher ruminatively, placing the tips of his fingers together. 'There's no income from timber – there isn't much left – and the rents are minimal because there are only a few cottages. A big estate like this carries a cross from generation to generation in the cottages it provides free of rent and rates for its staff and pensioners. Anyone who's worked here up to fifteen years or more – and many have worked more than forty years – is given a cottage free for their lifetime, including their wife's lifetime. That includes maintenance, which in the old days wasn't worth very much but now is worth a great deal. We still carry about twenty-nine or thirty, which relieves the State of a certain amount of responsibility.'

On top of that there are about sixteen farm-workers' cottages; three for the gamekeepers, fifteen for management, including the farm manager, three or four for the garden staff, including the head gardener's house, 500 yards from Harewood House itself, six for the foresters and Ussher's own, a substantial Georgian dwelling near the stable block, once used as a brew-house – 'when we dug up the drains we found they were all white, salt-glazed pipes'. The house has six bedrooms – more than the owner of Harewood can boast nowadays, although his four have dressing rooms attached. But the agent at Harewood has always lived in style; a generation or two ago he had a big house in the village with six to eight bedrooms, a horse and carriage (and later on garaging for four cars) and a fifty-acre farm, and his household staff included both a coachman and a butler.

'Our main effort now is to run the farm as profitably as we can, and the house with its Bird Garden, butterflies and so on, the idea being that if those two can generate sufficient cash flow to at least balance the books on the other side (there's nine and a half miles of wall around the park which has to be repaired, that's just one of the unknown factors which has to come out of Lord Harewood's income), then we can keep our heads above water. But can anyone on the big estates do this for very much longer, when inflation asks the owner to pump a higher rate each year into the pool? At the moment, the shortfall on Harewood House is £30,000 a year; we have not been able to balance the books in the last ten years.'

Ussher reports directly to Lord Harewood, the only member of staff to do so. (He is also the only member of staff to have possession of the huge key to the front door of Harewood.) 'I get his instructions and where I don't, I make up my own mind. I don't make any decisions for the heads of department; in any organization, once you delegate you hope they'll get on with it; I just keep a benevolent eye on things. I see most of them daily, particularly Richard Cobbald, the farm manager, and David Wrench. Then there's John Lister, the clerk of works – he might see me about anything from someone's clogged kitchen sink to the roof of the house falling in. The head forester, Bert Meredith, sees me about anything to do with his chaps, who do quite a lot of work that isn't necessarily forestry, such as mending roads and fences. Then I run the domestic side of Harewood House – not the social side any more, though I did that for the Princess Royal, but they've got a very capable secretary now who looks after all that. Lady Harewood always arranges who's coming to stay, when they come and go and what they eat (he decides what they drink), but I run the household accounts and sign the cheques. I also do all the hiring and firing; I've just appointed a new butler. Then I had to find a new curator for the Bird Garden because the chap who created it in 1969, Peter Brown, was leaving to go to Australia. I found Bill Timmis at Chester Zoo and introduced him to Lord Harewood.'

Typical events in Ussher's day might include three hours with an expert from Christie's looking at some iron railings which were at Chesterfield House in London before it was pulled down in the 1930s and which may now go to a National Trust property in Sussex; chairing a meeting of the Game Conservancy in York; approving someone's application for a charity's sponsored walk round the park; settling a dispute about an overflowing drain; selling a cottage or paddock; giving the *Yorkshire Post* a comment about a council decision to put up traffic lights on the Leeds–Harrogate road in front of Harewood's main gates. Once a month or so, he will go to London to see the Harewoods' legal adviser and 'financial overlord', Philip Byam-Cook.

Receding all the time, like Gatsby's green light at the end of Scott Fitzgerald's novel, is the elusive goal of balancing the books – keeping this house afloat, leaky with heavy maintenance costs, which are boosted each month by inflation and the frightening rise in fuel prices. 'The situation *is* getting worse,' admits Ussher, 'but one must be fair, one must be prepared to turn the non-income-producing units of the estate either into a better investment or into liquid cash. Ten years ago a cottage falling vacant would have been worth £1500 – now it's £15,000. And although inflation has forced the cost of everything else up, it's better to have £15,000 to pump back into the estate than £1500, which wouldn't have gone very far even then.

'The farm makes a substantial trading profit, yes, but like everyone else in the big farming business today, you have this terrible cash flow problem. A combine harvester which you only need for three weeks in the year now costs £25,000, and borrowings for that sort of thing have become enormous. The profit is on valuations, not on cash flow, which is nothing like large enough to feed back. This morning's milk cheque, for instance' – and he riffles through a pile of papers on his blotter – 'was £33,365 for the month. We banked another £11,533, that's roughly £44,000 – but I wrote cheques yesterday for at least £44,000.

'It's all these things that have to be carried. It costs £2000 to audit the house-opening accounts alone. Our total admissions were almost exactly the same this year as last – 256,233 against 256,030, though we put the price up a bit and spending per head has gone up a bit too. So after VAT we've banked £53,339 against £46,827 to the same date last year. Wear and tear and maintenance, that comes to about £26,000 on the house, gate and park in a year – about £18,000 on the house alone.

'We are recognized as a building of Class I historic interest, important enough to qualify for tax purposes as Case I, Schedule D – that is, the expenses against your admission money are allowable for tax. The problem is, how far does this go? Heating and lighting of the house, where justified for proper care of the contents, is obviously all right. But we have a standing joke about the front door mat – how many times is it worn out by Lord Harewood, how many times by visitors? Well, he pays his share – 1/47,000 or whatever, and he also pays his own share of anything to do with private gardening, but you can hardly say that he's got to pay for looking out of the window over gardens which, after all, are maintained for the benefit of the general public. . . .

'But at the end of the day the administration, heating and lighting of the house, upkeep of the gardens and drive and so on do produce a shortfall. Now what price do you set your ticket at in order to get rid of the shortfall? This is an immensely complex problem. It's no good saying that Covent Garden would make a profit if you charged everybody £157 a seat, because nobody would go to the opera. The same thing applies to Harewood House. And Lord Harewood has always said that if you have 265,000 people wanting to come here, not necessarily to see the house or the Bird Garden but just to be out in the country because they live in a concrete jungle, you can't charge them a lot of money just to come into the grounds. So we try to keep our park entry down to a minimum.

'I don't suppose anyone in the great houses has ever really balanced the books. Subsidy has to come in. You just can't tell the ordinary people of Leeds and Bradford that it'll cost them one pound to come into the park and three pounds to see the house and Bird Garden.'

The money that underpins most of this complex structure comes from the farm, though in practice there is little actual cross-fertilization. The farm has been managed for twenty years by Richard Cobbald, who came on personal recommendation, a good practical record and because he knew something about Red Poll cattle. The Princess Royal's herd was ideal for an establishment like Harewood because, being hornless, they could run with the racehorses in the paddock without damaging them.

'Cobbald built the farm up from a small herd of Red Polls to this vast business enterprise. He does the buying and selling of the cows and so on, and he has three sub-managers under him. One used to run 400 acres in Lincolnshire but chose to come here at a lower managerial level. All our cows are kept indoors and fed on silage all year round, which causes a bit of a problem with the slurry – it has to be pumped out somewhere. Today after lunch I found the whole thing had overflowed all over the road. Lord Harewood absolutely hates this sort of thing; he says, why must I put on gumboots every time I go outside the house? That's fair enough, but the latest scheme for pumping all the stuff somewhere else, squeezing out the solids and pumping the liquid back on to the land would cost £50,000 for starters.

'Twenty-five years ago we had three men and a girl looking after thirty-three cows and their progeny – now we have five men looking after five hundred, milking them three times a day with complicated machinery. The dairy cattle produce nearly half a million pounds' worth of milk a year, gross, but it costs a whacking lot to do it. The farm buildings are on the slope of a hill in the middle of a wood, so they're not easy to modernize. The farmworkers may not be at the top of the national wages tree, but a lot of them have free houses and some kind of travelling allowance, and with a season like we've just had, everything wet and cold and late (we lost twenty-one sheep in one day last winter), it's easy to find a chap topping £100 a week with twenty or thirty hours overtime. The turnover on the farm in 1977 was £597,000 and in 1978 it was £618,000, but the wages bill was £105,000 and feed for the pigs and sheep £359,000.'

Vagaries of weather apart, there is probably little that Ussher and his managers can do to improve the farm's efficiency, but on the house-opening side, the search is constantly on for the innovation that will bring in more of the public, and a watchful eye is kept on what others in the stately homes business are doing. 'We haven't any major competitors close by – important ones like Castle Howard and Newby are far enough away; in fact, we're usually in close cooperation. But it's important to have something interesting to keep people coming. You mustn't ever have them saying, 'Oh we've been there, we've seen the furniture, it's the same as it was last time.' One must accept that it's a day out for the family and it's got to be different. Like every stately home, we've been through the gamut of considering big zoos, safari parks, golf courses, motor-racing circuits. But if you go into that realm, you may be destroying the very thing they've come to see. If you make an adventure playground out of wood and landscape it properly, or have tropical birds in the garden, that's different because it fits in. Eventually, we'd like to have a pet zoo where children can actually walk among the animals and stroke them. We've had some schools here from the poorer parts of Leeds where the kids have never in their lives walked on grass that wasn't in a public park, and very seldom even that. If they were allowed to stroke a calf or something, think how immensely exciting that would be for them.'

Promising sidelines often have to be scrapped because the profit won't be worth the investment, or the market is wrong. A plan to make pâté and game specialities foundered because it would have cost too much (£60,000 minimum), there were problems over where to prepare and sell it, and it might have taken profit away from other items sold such as the Wedgwood. Mrs Ussher is the buyer for the Harewood shops and able to advise on such matters. Ussher did once try selling game, plucked and ready for the oven, but found so many people came to the estate office asking questions about cooking the pheasants that 'it would have kept someone downstairs five minutes at a time talking about this damned pheasant, and then they'd have wanted to bring the other one back if they didn't like it. So we gave that one up.'

One established crowd-puller, the traction engine rally, had to be abandoned because the profit on attendance worked out at precisely a penny a head. Besides that, the weight of the engines was compacting the soil of the park so firmly that five or six years later Geoff Hall finds the rainwater won't soak through and the ground will have to be aerated with a special spiked roller.

The exigencies of pulling in the tourists must, after all, never impair the star attraction, whether it is a question of rescuing dying grass or discreetly covering a patch of wall tapestry with clear plastic sheeting where inquisitive fingers have touched and rubbed the silk to a cobweb. For the sole purpose of all this cash-generating activity, the hub around which everything revolves, from the production of half a million gallons of milk to the sale of 5p postcards, is the survival of Harewood House and its uniqueness as an English country house. Ussher suspects that no government would actually let Harewood die for lack of cash. 'But, like every other stately home, so long as the owner is prepared to live in it and somehow or other support it where needed, no matter how much it deprives his heirs of some future inheritance, that will have to go on, but with increasingly limited funds.'

Half a mile away, as the light fades over the park, the last visitors are beginning their forty-minute circuit of the house. In the Butterfly House, children press their noses against the glass cages, intent on the immobile Monarchs with their red-gold wings patched with brown, and riveted by the incessantly restless anthill and its labouring inhabitants. In the Bird Garden, working men's families from Leeds loudly discuss the peculiarities of the penguins – one hasn't moved on its rock for an hour; another is hooting mournfully at the darkening sky; a third picks its way over the stones by the pool, stubby wings held out stiffly, like an elderly waiter with corns. A couple from Bradford drink tea out of paper cups in the old stables, picturing the scene over seventy years ago. She says, 'Just think, the horses and carriages, all jingling, it must have been marvellous'. Dryly, he reminds her, 'And we'd have been doing the mucking out!'

In the two shops, they are cashing up the day's takings from the Wedgwood plates painted with Harewood scenes, the pottery mugs and the prints of Wharfedale. It comes to £223.80. Tom McGrath collects it and takes it up to security along with the admission money, £327.32, and the house takings, £51.40. The Bird Garden closes; nobody under a briar bush tonight, just the lonely calls of the expatriates and the contented rumble of native doves. Last off the premises is Geoff Hall, who seals the terrace and locks the gates – 'I like to do it myself, then I know it's done.' He has been worrying about the inexplicable theft last week of two stone owls from the terrace.

In the security room lie bags containing £602.52 spent by 532 visitors – not bad for a cool, showery Friday at the beginning of the season and well up on the comparable day last year (£528). Above Barry's imperious High Victorian skyline, the Lascelles banner flaps idly in the evening breeze (when they leave on Tuesday it will be replaced by the Union Jack). The banner is significant, for without the regular involvement of a family, the domestic continuity of three hundred years and a staff still more of a country-house ménage than an official payroll, it would be an arid museum, beautiful but soulless and no longer related to the life of this particular patch of England.

Down by the lake, a shadowy figure paces slowly, intent on something in the night air. It is Geoff Hall. At the end of a seven-day week his greatest pleasure is still to come out after supper and sniff the night-time scents – 'it's the best time for the aromatic flowers.' This proprietary attitude on the part of the people who work there is ultimately what sets a house like Harewood apart from the French château or Italian palazzo – where is the state-paid curator who would want to spend his evenings checking on the progress of his night-scented stocks? But even as Geoff Hall strolls his garden by night, decisions are being taken thousands of miles away in the Middle East which will give the intricate mechanism of the industrial world another inflationary twist, and the effects will not take long to penetrate this quiet park. The spiralling cost of oil will not only raise the price of everything supplied through or dependent on it, here as everywhere else, but it will also stop an unguessed-at number of people from climbing into their cars for a casual day out at a stately home. In Neville Ussher's office, the sums for next year will soon have to be done again; the already mortgaged future shortens by an unknown number of weeks, months or years. At Harewood tonight, however, no such problems yet disturb the peace of the Yorkshire spring countryside. Tomorrow is another day on the farm, in the forests, of selling pottery and postcards and a family's heritage in forty minutes.

11

A Heritage in Pawn?

David Henry George Lascelles, who was born in 1950 and in the fullness of years will become the eighth Earl of Harewood, is a man very much of his time: classless, industrious, concerned about conservation and the social purposes of land ownership in the last quarter of the twentieth century. Tall, rangily built, dark-moustached, he runs his own film production company in Bath, making chiefly documentaries on West Country subjects. His two younger brothers by Lord Harewood's first marriage are both in the pop music business – one as a musician, the other as a record company executive. David Lascelles lives in a village north of Bath with his wife Margaret and three small children. If he has to stay in London it is with one of his brothers or at his mother's house; he is probably the first Viscount Lascelles not to enjoy a town house of his own, or the facilities of a grand Harewood mansion in the West End, apart from his father, whose early adult years before inheritance were spent in wartime service. But his reaction to that thought is a surprised chuckle; it is clearly not one that has entered his head.

'I've no particular nostalgia for the past,' he says, and he does not feel in the least possessive about the famous house that will one day be his responsibility. He has, however, a very strongly developed and contemporary version of *noblesse oblige* – not only is Harewood important to keep going as 'a bit of history', but perhaps even more so as 'a facility – somewhere for people to go; it's a marvellous place for a day out.' To Lascelles, the attraction of Harewood, in which he spends two or three days a month on average, sometimes longer if he can do some film work at the same time, is primarily the countryside it sits in; the woods, lake and birds. He has vestiges of the sporting tastes of his ancestors, though he claims he is by nature neither a landowner nor a farmer. There is nothing he likes better than to go out with the agent, Neville Ussher, a gun and a dog for a spot of rough shooting on the estate. But more often he derives his satisfactions from the peculiarly clear, bright days of winter, from watching birds congregate on the lake – it has become something of a bird sanctuary, he says, since the Bird Garden opened in 1970 – and enjoying the solitude of the woods. The house is an inextricable part of that particular landscape, but 'it's not the sort of place I'd want to live', he says simply. This is partly a matter of logistics; it is no easy matter with three small children to come and go between the first-floor family apartments and the private section of the gardens – involving a three-part journey by lift, passageways and a dash across the terrace – especially at the height of the house-opening season. The presence of the public doesn't actively bother him, but it is obviously not a private and easy way to live. Lascelles, when he becomes earl, will probably choose to have a house somewhere else on the estate where the family can live more informally.

He does see a strong case for conservation – the word his father always stresses over preservation, which implies something static rather than evolving – and for the necessity to save historic houses for reasons not only of history but of the social amenity such places provide, especially in areas like Harewood, which is encircled by four great industrial conurbations; Leeds, Bradford, Wakefield and Halifax. Obviously, as he says, families owning such houses cannot expect consideration from any government simply to enable them to maintain a style of life they have always enjoyed – although this would be true of very few families today and certainly not of the Lascelles, who all lead busy lives elsewhere. Indeed, the family connection in his view is fairly irrelevant now, except in so far as it enhances the interest of visiting the house. But there is a limit to the further amount of land which could be sold off to keep such a closely interdependent estate financially viable. In Harewood's case, its future owner thinks, 'it only works all of a piece, and it wouldn't work if the place shrank any more.' This wholeness and interdependence of the various parts of the estate go right down to the miniature social welfare system which is operated for retired workers; something which, in its community closeness and concern for the individual, should commend itself even to political opponents of land ownership, though how much longer that system can continue against rising financial pressures remains to be seen.

The family does, from time to time, discuss contingency plans against the various future paths tax legislation could take. If it became necessary, some kind of family trust would probably be devised to ensure that the parts of the whole were held together; probably, says Lord Harewood, requiring some kind of charitable status to achieve its aims, the kind of family company trust which used to exist having long since lost its advantages. Such a trust would change little in the day-to-day administration of the estate, being run largely by the kind of people who effectively run Harewood now; lawyers, agents and professional advisers of various kinds under the 'chairmanship' of Lord Harewood. Plans are also periodically reviewed as to further works of art which might one day have to be sold to keep the encroaching tide of costs at bay; there are some which Lord Lascelles says he would not want to see leave the house, but others which have a relatively brief historical connection with the family. The Titian fell into that category, despite the subsequent outcry over the prospect of it leaving Britain: the eventual outcome, with the National Gallery being enabled to buy it back for the nation, was seen by the Harewood family as something of a coup. Lascelles remembers attending the sale when he was twenty-one; the atmosphere was so heightened and unreal that he lost all sense of time passing and to this day cannot recall if it was long or short.

Even at the age of thirty, Lascelles had seen great changes in Harewood, both the house and the village. As a child, he remembered, the family quarters changed several times. The Library then, in the Princess Royal's lifetime, was the main family sitting room; a warm, hospitable place, 'all wood and leather, the sort of room I like', with a series of small sitting areas to break up its expanse. Unlike his father, and rather to his regret, he did not play village cricket with the local boys; that pleasant custom seems to have died out after the Second World War, along with the village choir, once twenty-two strong, in which all the estate workers' children used to have to take part. Geoff Hall, former head gardener to the estate, recalled that for his annual efforts in the choir he was paid 'the princely sum of two shillings and sixpence', which he received with some ceremony each Easter from the vicar, then a relative of the Lascelles family. Choir practices took place in the village hall twice a week and that meant a total of five miles' walking for young Geoff Hall, whose family lived a mile and a quarter outside the village.

The cricket pitch still lies in Harewood park, just in front of

Admission Control, and Cliff Lancaster, a retired farmworker, re-membered how they used to bring down trestle tables from the house and lay out 'feasts of teas'. George Lascelles, the present earl, is remem-bered as a good bat but a pugnacious lad who used to get involved in punch-ups with the village boys. Derek Deakin, whose family ran the village garage, recalled seeing one of these fights taking place only yards from the Princess Royal in her deckchair: she placidly continued with her knitting as if nothing were happening. The passing of the cricket matches is regretted by the old-timers as yet another example of present-day apathy and lack of community spirit. Originally, the village boys had to cut the grass before they could use the pitch, but later on Lord Harewood had it mown for them; even so, the interest had gone.

Harewood village has perhaps changed faster in the last five to ten years than at any time since Carr laid out his model terraces. In that it is not alone – 'it's happening to villages all over England,' says Lord Las-celles, in whose childhood twenty-odd years ago nearly all the Harewood villagers worked on or were connected with the estate. Now the well-heeled middle-class commuters are moving in – lawyers from Harrogate, businessmen from Leeds, a Swedish restaurateur – and new houses in the village are reputed to be selling for as much as £100,000 each. In 1976 Lord Harewood sold three acres adjoining the park and the estate office to a Leeds developer, Arncliffe Holdings, with the stipu-lation that the design of any development must be approved by him. This was done, and the new buildings, known as the Mews, blend decently enough with their eighteenth-century surroundings, although older inhabitants predictably dislike their existence. Some of these are picturesquely blunt in their condemnation of what is happening to the village. 'It's the deadest place now,' said Alfie Bryant, a retired farm labourer in his seventies whose life since boyhood has been spent work-ing the land round Harewood. 'In the old days they had no money but they had heart in their bellies. Now they've money but no heart.' In his opinion the incomers in their expensive new houses in the Mews are 'no good to Harewood – it would have been better for Harewood if they'd never come. If they'd put cows or horses on that three acres it would have done more good for the village.' In a memorable image, fished up perhaps from his distant childhood, he castigated the new commuters as 'like a baking-powder drink – all fizz'.

Lloyd George, who doubtless still ranks high in the demonology of England's remaining landowners, has generally been blamed as the first to destroy village life by introducing the taxation which effectively broke up the great estates. What he began, of course, was completed by the social upheaval of two world wars, the flight from the land into industry and the inexorable intermingling of urban and country ways by the car, telephone, radio and television. It is undoubtedly the presence of a historic house and working estate, however truncated, that has enabled Harewood village and others like it to retain much of their original character. Without them, a village in such close proximity to industrial cities would long since have been swallowed up in the kind of notorious ribbon suburbia that began to disfigure the countryside in the 1920s. There is, of course, always the danger that the village may *look* the same, but with progressive 'gentrification' and the passing of many working functions, become little more than a shell; this, plainly, is what many of the older agricultural workers feel has happened to Harewood. The Square, for instance, used to be the bustling heart of the village with a cluster of shops; cobbler, draper, butcher. Now it stands elegant, but empty. The last butcher, Illingworth – a name rooted in Harewood for generations – moved out in the mid-1970s, and the village now has only one small general shop and a surgery with a visiting doctor.

Time has made other changes. The castle, to which the fifth earl and Lady Florence used to take a weekly stroll – the estate workers had to sweep the path every Friday in preparation – is now derelict and dangerous. Lord Harewood has placed it off-limits and the grassy rides which used to give access to it have been allowed to grow over. But it is still a haunting, elusive presence; motorists glancing to the right halfway up Harewood Bank can catch a glimpse of the two ruined towers, jagged fingers pointing skyward out of a grove of trees. The village children still dare each other to climb the broken masonry and there have been tragedies on the 100-foot-high walls. One village girl aged eleven fell years ago from the top and is now, in middle age, paralysed with sclerosis as a result. The church, where seven generations of Lascelles are interred in the family vault, is being restored by volunteers from the Redundant Church Users' Association; it ceased to be used for worship in the mid-1970s and is now a listed monument. In the spring of 1980 new lead was put in the roof and the stone fabric repaired here and there. The sculpted effigies from the six famous tombs commemorating the fifteenth-century lords of Harewood Castle were laid out incongruously on rough wooden trestle tables with large castors, looking for all the world like immobile patients on hospital stretchers, while workers strengthened the floor of the church, which had become unsafe to bear the weight of the tombs. Their stone features, exquisitely carved, look calmly down the centuries as though medieval England were just the day before yesterday. The Ryther features are worn by time but those of the Redmans and Sir William Gascoigne remain sharp and delicate. The feeling of a time warp is intensified by the list of vicars – only thirty-two of them from Father Laur de Wath in 1354 to H.H. Griffith, the incumbent from 1928 to 1974. Harewood church today is hidden away in a thicket up a dirt track to the right of the drive that takes visitors through Admission Control, and special permission was required to visit it during the restoration work.

'The English country house is as archaic as the osprey,' wrote James Lees-Milne in 1974, the year that Dr Roy Strong at the Victoria and Albert Museum mounted a devastatingly graphic exhibition charting the destruction this century of hundreds of examples of this uniquely English contribution to domestic architecture. No exact figures are available, but as Lees-Milne commented, the revolution has been swift. 'It has taken a mere lifetime to wipe out an institution of four centuries.' Around four hundred houses were demolished in the years immediately following the First World War and, with the exception of the period 1939–45, when Britain's energies were directed elsewhere, it has been calculated that the assault on country houses accounted for an average of thirteen demolitions every year between 1930 and 1955. Roy Strong estimated in 1974 that about 250 houses 'of architectural and historic importance' had gone since 1945, and that only about 1000 were left in private hands. *Burke's Landed Gentry* was more pessimistic, putting the figure at 400 destroyed between 1952 and 1964. Yorkshire lost more than any other county – twenty-three in West Yorkshire alone. 'The Twenties, Thirties, Forties and Fifties are black decades in our architectural history,' wrote John Harris in a contribution to the book accompanying the V&A exhibition. 'It was comparable to the Reformation, and the sadness is that it was not necessary.'

The last three decades have certainly witnessed a change in such cavalier attitudes to irreplaceable buildings. In the 1980s, when a country-house owner wants to pull down a distinguished property on the grounds that it has become unsafe or that he cannot afford to repair its crumbling fabric, there is outrage in the land, and the Secretary of State for the Environment is urged to slap a preservation order on it, as even the Secretary of State's Cabinet colleague, Francis Pym, found to his discomfiture when he tried to demolish an architectural white elephant on his family estate. The Wedgwood china company likewise found its hands tied, pending a public inquiry, over the fate of Barlaston Hall, a magnificent but semi-derelict eighteenth-century mansion in the Potteries, once connected (but only briefly, since the 1930s) with the Wedgwood family. The disadvantage of this display of public spirit is that the building in question may decay irrevocably for lack of repair. On the other hand, one can argue irrefutably that it is never possible to repair a hole in the ground.

Decay, of course, can take many forms, and the process may be so insidious that no one notices it – even so, something is going for ever. An editorial in *Country Life* in 1974 expressed it well: 'It is not in the nature of houses to come to an end with a bang. They go downhill, the pictures and furniture follow the books and silver to the saleroom, dry rot gets a grip on the roof and the garden goes to seed.' The Gowers Report of 1950 decided that 'the owner of the house is almost always the best person to preserve it', and without the system of primogeniture in England, many estates would certainly have disappeared years ago, their houses gone or changed utterly, their collections dispersed among the dealers' showrooms of three continents. Yet if the owner cannot keep the place going, or tries to run it as it was never intended to be run, what then? It has been argued that the worst enemy of the country house, even more than taxation, is the disappearance of the self-sufficient community of domestic workers; the country house can survive without the butler, the footman and the lady's maid, but not without the estate carpenter and that useful jack of all trades who used to be known as 'the odd man'. Without them, all those little depredations of wear and tear which individually are not important enough to warrant expert and costly repair by craftsmen summoned from London, cumulatively eat away at the fabric. In the old days, they would have been spotted and put right by the house staff as they happened. It is hard to know how this particular loss can be made good. Harewood is one of the lucky houses in still having its house carpenter, in his brown linen coat, prowling around with a sharp eye for a crack in the panelling there, a warping floorboard here, a bit of veneer splitting off the Chippendale somewhere else . . . but many others are not.

The weight of English history certainly favours the survival of the country house. It is bound up with the English subconscious, from the time when, as the social historian G.E. Mingay wrote, the countryside and its values dominated the city, not the other way round. 'It was in the mansion-houses of the gentry, not the market towns, that political decisions were taken, economic projects planned, the local community governed, and the cultural life of the age flourished. And the very permanence of the country house itself, its ancient halls studded by darkening ancestral portraits, instilled the sense of continuity and stability that was so strong an element in the squirearchy. . . . By the later nineteenth century the gentry were economically, socially and politically in retreat. But they survived.' And he quoted from Chester Kirby, author of a work called *The English Country Gentleman*, to indicate why: 'They did not understand the new ways of life, but they had unlimited experience of governing. They were not efficient, but then many of them worked for nothing! They were not always very industrious, but what they did was all to the good, for they had nothing else to do. In short, tradition gave them an influence over all England, which accepted the notion that they were born to govern; it endowed them with a collective experience, handed on from father to son; it supplied them with an attitude of mastery, an easy self-assurance which in itself gave them an enormous advantage over any competitor.' Unlike the experience of other countries, England's continued acceptance of the landowning caste and its values was helped by the fact that land had always been seen by English owners in productive terms rather than as a source of power and prestige. This is truer than ever today, when most landowners – certainly the younger ones – regard their estates, if not their homes as well, as commercial enterprises to be directed and managed as efficiently as any business. The young Duke of Roxburghe, speaking on BBC television's 'Man Alive' programme in 1979, said: 'The estate almost ran itself in the old days. Now it's a full-time job, like a big business.'

But the English attitude towards country life of the stately kind goes much deeper than mere tolerance or even admiration for a species which has adapted skilfully to the industrialized, relatively classless world of the late twentieth century. For one thing, class does remain a very potent current in English life – less so in the Celtic culture of Scotland, Wales or Ireland – even if it is submerged deeper than it used to be. People are as fascinated as they ever were, if not as awed, by the symbols of privilege, and the dream of the successful manufacturer, property developer or City financier is still, as in the days of Thomas Brassey, Thomas Armstrong and the first Rothschilds, to own a country house and some land. It seems curiously appropriate that the Lutyens house

built in 1909 at Sonning-on-Thames for Edward Hudson, founder of
Country Life, the periodical which has done so much to foster that
dream, should now be owned by one of the most successful entrepreneurs of the last twenty years, Nigel Broackes, founder of the
property-based conglomerate Trafalgar House, whose interests stretch
from the liner *Queen Elizabeth 2* and the London Ritz to Express
Newspapers. Harry Hyams, the property tycoon who built Centre
Point and whose fortune was one put at £50 million, lives a secluded
private life at sixteenth-century Ramsbury Manor in Wiltshire. There
are dozens of similar examples. 'Country houses', wrote John Cornforth of *Country Life*, 'are part of the deep-seated British preference for
a country life, with its feeling for landscape, its belief in the satisfactions
and responsibilities of landowning and its enthusiasm for gardening
and forestry.' On a humbler economic level, Ronald Blythe, author of
the hugely successful *Akenfield*, a social documentary of a composite
East Anglian village, noted: 'The townsman . . . in Britain has always
regarded urban life as just a temporary necessity. One day he will find a
cottage on the green and "real values".' Anthony Sampson in his *New
Anatomy of Britain* (1971) observed 'the basic fascination of town
dwellers with the land'; and the way that the village-based radio serial
'The Archers', originally intended as a kind of documentary service to
farmers, has become a national institution is eloquent proof of that.

George Orwell, that sharp-eyed outsider who cut so perceptively
through the layers of British social attitudes, wrote in the egalitarian
morning of Attlee's England, in 1947: 'The ambition to be a country
gentleman, to own and administer land and draw at least a part of your
income from rent, has survived every change. So it comes that each new
wave of parvenus, instead of simply replacing the existing ruling class,
has adopted its habits, intermarried with it and, after a generation or
two, become indistinguishable from it. . . . And the comparative integrity of the British ruling class . . . is probably bound up with their idea of
themselves as feudal landowners. This outlook is shared by considerable sections of the middle class. Nearly everyone who can afford to do
so sets up as a country gentleman, or at least makes some effort in that
direction. The manor house with its park and its walled gardens re-
appears in reduced form in the stockbroker's weekend cottage, in the
suburban villa with its lawn and herbaceous border, perhaps even in the
potted nasturtiums on the window-sill of the Bayswater flat. This widespread daydream is undoubtedly snobbish, it has tended to stabilize

class distinctions and has helped to prevent the modernization of English agriculture; but it is mixed up with a kind of idealism, a feeling that style and tradition are more important than money.'

Such middle-class daydreams cannot, however, account for the huge popularity of country-house visiting as a mass-market leisure activity. It has grown to enormous proportions, from the two or three million visitors historic homes were attracting after their first decade open to the public, to the 53 million recorded in 1979 – admittedly to a much longer list of places and with 10 million coming from overseas, but still a domestic figure equivalent to 78 per cent of Britain's population. The appeal is obviously compounded of many factors: the pleasure of urban dwellers in the unspoilt countryside which the great estates provide, ancillary attractions like Lord Montagu's National Motor Museum at Beaulieu, the lions at Longleat and the Woburn zoo and sideshows, the opportunity for a glimpse of how the upper tenth once lived and – with the growth of popular antiques programmes on television – the chance to feast on some of the finest works of art in Britain in their original settings. Mark Girouard, the country-house historian, has suggested that one reason for the absorbing interest of these houses is that 'they are at once infinitely remote and just round the corner; the vast and elaborate social edifice only crumbled finally a few decades ago.' And Girouard added: 'I myself can remember, in the Forties and Fifties, being called by house maids or footmen carrying brass cans of hot water, and taking chamber pots in the bedroom for granted and using them without second thoughts. This now sounds like saying that I remember having had to use flint arrowheads'. Dr Roy Strong, director of the V&A, commented in *The Destruction of the Country House* that, although the system of society for which country houses were created has disappeared, 'we are left with the superb visual apparatus. . . . The great houses of England and their occupants represent a continuity within our society.' Country house owners, he concluded, 'are the hereditary custodians of what was one of the most vital forces of cultural creation in our history.'

By and large, these custodians are working hard and ingeniously to maintain the sap of life in this cultural force, if not by the tourist trade alone, by finding other means of adapting the use of their ancestral homes to modern demand as settings for executive meetings, full-blown conferences, product launches, seminars or commercial banquets. Lord Brocket, of the Elizabethan Brocket Hall near Welwyn, and the Marquess of Northampton, of Castle Ashby, are just two owners who have gone all out for the business market. Lord Northampton's father, the sixth marquess, joined in the great land sales after the First World War and his letter to *The Times* about large-scale landowning being unpopular was thought then to be socially significant. 'Landowning on a large scale is now generally felt to be a monopoly and is consequently unpopular.' Unlike many of his peers, however, he invested the proceeds of his land sales very shrewdly in equities and in later years was able not only to buy back most of his original estates (one farm was bought back in 1969 exactly fifty years after it was sold), but to add to them. The old marquess, who lived to be ninety-two and thus comfortably outwitted the tentacles of capital transfer tax, used to describe himself in *Who's Who* as 'owns 10,000 acres'. The Northamptons now have more land than they ever had, and the present marquess, who was born in 1946 (and does *not* list his land holdings in *Who's Who*), enjoys the possession of two beautiful stately homes. He lives with his third wife in the exquisite Tudor Compton Wynyates in Warwickshire. Sixteenth-century Castle Ashby, which is somewhat off the tourist track, has been turned, after much professional research into possible market uses, into a 'centre for all occasions', its ground-floor rooms refurbished at a cost of £500,000 for anything from a directors' meeting to a seminar on salesmanship to a wedding reception. Wiring for all the gadgetry of modern conferences is cleverly hidden beneath a join in the carpet of the portrait-lined Reynolds Room; first-rate 'English country house cooking' is laid on, and Lord Northampton is available in person, if required, at no extra cost – or so the initial publicity went.

The young inheritors of the late twentieth century would surprise Orwell, who wrote in 1940: 'They [the ruling class] are not wicked, or not altogether wicked; they are merely unteachable. Only when their money and power are gone will the younger among them begin to grasp what century they are living in.' The richest of the young aristocrats, the sixth Duke of Westminster, paradoxically owns no famous ancestral seat, the family's grandiose 1870 creation, Eaton Hall by Alfred Waterhouse, having been demolished in 1962. But those who do own such properties are mostly highly aware of the need to make them work for the century they are living in. Most are also conscious of the value of maintaining a family connection, however tenuous, to give life and interest to the house, whatever its function. Not many have followed the example of Lord Brooke and gone to live abroad, after selling Warwick

Castle to Madame Tussaud's, a subsidiary of the S. Pearson group controlled by Lord Cowdray, or of Lord Rosebery, who put up the contents of Mentmore Towers for sale in a much-publicized auction in 1977 and subsequently sold the house to the followers of the Maharishi Mahesh Yogi, founder of the transcendental meditation cult. Ian Fraser Martin, silver steward at Chatsworth, the Duke of Devonshire's magnificent Derbyshire seat, used to work at the Devonshires' other famous property, Hardwick Hall, which is run by the National Trust, and vastly prefers the atmosphere at Chatsworth: 'You feel different if they're at home,' he says. Although the Harewoods usually manage to slip through the Entrance Hall without being recognized, the sight of the black and gold family standard flying above the north portico gives an added quiver of interest to a trip around the house. 'Is the Duke at home?' people ask Jimmy Nairn, head gamekeeper to the Duke of Roxburghe.

Owners may not all be as passionately devoted to their historic bricks and mortar as the Marquess of Bath, whose younger son Lord Christopher Thynne has said on television that if it came to a choice for his father between shooting a son or seeing the house burn he, Christopher, would 'start running'. Indeed, Lord Bath's heir, the pony-tailed Viscount Weymouth, believes in abolishing titles, wants independence for Wessex and will probably run Longleat in a very different way from his father when it comes to his turn. Viscount Lascelles, it seems, will run Harewood in much the same way as his father, though without necessarily maintaining a home in it. The physical problems of preserving country houses may be relieved by changing legislation as much as the tax burden of their owners risks being increased. The fledgling National Heritage Fund, established in 1980, has already done good work within its limitations – it can aid purchase or National Trust endowment, but not pay for repairs. But in the end, whether historic houses like Harewood, Longleat, Castle Ashby and the others live or die rests with the owner. Individuals – men of vision, egotism, wealth, taste, power or a permutation of those qualities – built them and breathed life into them. Each house was unique and none could ever be built again. Individuals, not institutions or the state, remain the best hope for their survival.

Bibliography

Harewood House and Village

Barry, Alfred, *The Life of Sir Charles Barry* (London, 1867).

Borenius, Tancred, *The Harewood Collection* (London, 1936).

Gilbert, Christopher, *The Life and Work of Thomas Chippendale* (Cassell, London, 1978).

Greenwood, W., *The Redmans and the Levens of Harewood* (Kendal, 1905).

Jewell, John, *The Tourist's Companion or the History of the Antiquities of Harewood* (Leeds, 1819).

Jones, J., *History and Antiquities of Harewood* (London, 1859).

Mauchline, Mary, *Harewood House* (David and Charles, Newton Abbot, 1974).

Musgrave, E. I., *Harewood House* (English Life Publications, Derby, 1953).

Stroud, Dorothy, *Capability Brown* (Country Life Ltd, 1950).

Wheater, W., *Some Historic Mansions of Yorkshire* (Leeds, 1888).

Yorkshire and Wharfedale

Bogg, E., *A Thousand Miles in Wharfedale* (Leeds, 1892).

Bogg, E., *By the Banks of the Wharfe* (Leeds, 1921).

Fletcher, J.S., *Picturesque History of Yorkshire* (1900).

Fletcher, J.S., *The Making of Modern Yorkshire* (London, 1918).

Linstrum, Derek, *West Yorkshire Architects and Architecture* (Lund Humphries, London, 1978).

Lewis, C., *Wharfedale* (1937).

Mee, Arthur, *The King's England – Yorkshire*.

Pontefract, Ella, *Wharfedale* (Dent, London, 1938).

Singleton, Fred, *Industrial Revolution in Yorkshire* (1970).

Speight, H., *Upper Wharfedale* (London, 1900).

Speight, H., *Lower Wharfedale* (London, 1902).

Victoria County History, *Yorkshire*.

Walker, W., *Wharfdale* [sic] (Otley, 1813).

Country House and Estate History

Binney, Marcus and Strong, Roy, *The Destruction of the Country House* (Thames and Hudson, London, 1974).

Cornforth, John, *Country Houses in Britain: Can they Survive?* (Country Life, 1974).

Franklin, Jill, *The Gentleman's Country House and its Plan 1835–1914* (Routledge and Kegan Paul, London, 1981).

Girouard, Mark, *The Victorian Country House* (Yale University Press, 1971).

Girouard, Mark, *Life in the English Country House* (Yale University Press, 1978).

Hartcup, Adeline, *Below Stairs in the Great Country Houses* (Sigwick & Jackson, London, 1980).

Kent, N., *Hints to Landed Gentlemen* (1793).

Low, D., *Landed Property and the Economy of Estates* (1844).

Marshall, W., *On the Management of Landed Estates* (1806).

Morton, J.L., *The Resources of Estates* (1858).

Nevill, Ralph, *English Country House Life* (Methuen, London, 1925).

Sackville-West, V., *English Country Houses* (Collins, London, 1941).

General and Social History

Cathcart, Helen, *Anne and the Princess Royal* (London, W.H. Allen, 1973).

Farington, Joseph, *The Farington Diary, ed. James Grieg* (Hutchinson, London, 1922).

Hopkins, Harry, *The New Look: a social history of the Forties and Fifties in Britain* (London, Secker & Warburg, 1963).

Lees-Milne, James, *The Age of Adam* (1947).

Mingay, G.E., *English Landed Society in the Eighteenth Century* (Routledge & Kegan Paul, London, 1963).

Mingay, G.E., *The Gentry* (Longmans, London, 1976).

Mingay, G.E., *Rural Life in Victorian England* (Heinemann, London, 1977).

Pares, Richard, *The Historian's Business and Other Essays* (Oxford University Press, 1961).

Petrie, Sir Charles, *Scenes from Edwardian Life* (Eyre & Spottiswoode, London, 1965).

Plumb, J.H., *England in the Eighteenth Century* (Penguin, London, 1950).

Pope Hennessy, James, *Queen Mary* (London, Allen & Unwin, 1959).

Thompson, F.M.L., *English Landed Society in the Nineteenth Century* (Routledge & Kegan Paul, London, 1963).

Weiner, Martin J., *English Culture and the Decline of the Industrial Spirit 1850–1980* (Cambridge, 1981).

Files of *The Times, Yorkshire Post, Country Life.*

Index